I ALMOST BECAME ME

I ALMOST BECAME ME

A Memoir

CORY CALVIN

ISBN: 978-1-7339306-0-4

Names: Calvin, Cory, author.

Title: I almost became me : a memoir / Cory Calvin.

Description: Bryan, OH : Cory Calvin, 2019.

Identifiers: ISBN 978-1-7339306-0-4 (paperback) | ISBN 978-1-7339306-1-1 (ebook) | ISBN 978-1-7339306-2-8 (audiobook)

Subjects: LCSH: Gay men–Biography. | Coming out (Sexual orientation) | Closeted gays–Biography. | Life change events. | Families. | Self-actualization (Psychology)–Biography. | BISAC: BIOGRAPHY & AUTOBIOGRAPHY / LGBT. | BIOGRAPHY & AUTOBIOGRAPHY / Personal Memoirs.

Classification: LCC HQ75.8.C35 A3 2019 (print) | LCC HQ75.8.C35 (ebook) | DDC 306.7662/092–dc23.

I Almost Became Me is a work of nonfiction. Some names and identifying details have been changed.

www.IAlmostBecameMe.com
For orders or inquiries, please use the website.

DEDICATION

For my mother
I love you to the moon and back

RIP

ACKNOWLEDGMENTS

I AM SO grateful for all of the people who came before me to pave the way for LGBT+ rights. I wouldn't be able to share my story if it weren't for their brave leadership.

To my mother, for her unconditional love, for always believing in me and teaching me to follow my dreams no matter how big they are. And I am so honored to have been able to finish this book by her side before she passed away. Something I will never forget.

To Abby, Breanna, and Brandon, and to all of my family and friends, for their patience, love, and support (and for letting me sleep at their homes).

To Debi Havens, my spiritual and emotional mentor, for being a positive influence in my life.

To Azul Terronez, for coaching me throughout my book-writing journey and believing in me from the beginning.

To my incredible publishing team who helped me so much. Special thanks to Ann Maynard for her creative ideas to help develop my book and to find my voice as a new author; to Rochelle Deans for her flawless editing and assistance in polishing this manuscript; to Michael Rehder for the stunning cover design; and to Phillip Gessert for the creative visual interior design.

TABLE OF CONTENTS

1
THE DEVIL LIVES INSIDE OF YOU

THE DEVIL INSIDE

I'LL NEVER FORGET one of the last conversations I had with my father. It was extremely rare for my father and I to talk on the phone at all, let alone have any type of emotional conversation. In fact, we only spoke over the phone when my mother would make him pick up a second line and listen in on the conversation I had with her.

I had a thirty-minute drive ahead of me and decided to give my father a call, knowing it had been about a month since we last spoke around Christmas. I walked across the parking lot through the warm Florida air and opened the door to my black Cadillac. I sank into the soft leather driver's seat and slid on my thin-framed Ray-Bans.

It felt strange to dial my father's number on my cell phone. After several rings, my father answered. "Hey, Dad!" I said with a chipper tone.

My father returned my greeting somberly. For a moment, neither of us said anything else. My mother had left him five months ago. This time, it wasn't just a month-long separation like it had been ten years prior. It was for good.

After some brief chit-chat, I began to hear what sounded like my father crying. The only time I had ever heard him cry was when his father passed away twenty years ago. "What's wrong?" I asked with a concerned voice. I knew that my father's world was turning upside down. He was losing his marriage of thirty-four years and, more importantly, losing the crutch that held him up for most of his life.

My father sniveled into the phone. When he calmed down, he told me that he had a discussion with my mother during their divorce dialogue several months prior. And that it was about a conversation that I had had with my mother a long time ago. He wanted to know if a comment I made during that conversation was true.

My mind quickly raced through memories, trying to remember what I could have said to have him bring it up now, years later.

"Is it true that you told her that she should have divorced me a long time ago?" he asked slowly, calming down.

A wave of adrenaline flowed down from my head and knotted in my gut. It didn't feel like this was a question of facts, but instead it felt like a question to validate my love for him. Of everything we could be talking about, I was confused why this question was on top of his mind. This call definitely wasn't going to be a normal father-son catch-up conversation.

"Well, yes, Dad. I remember saying that. I remember being very scared in my bedroom when I was in the sixth grade, hearing you both yelling at each other in the living room. I told Mom later that evening when she tried to calm me down that you guys should divorce," I said and then paused, trying to gauge his reaction. Quick exhales came through the phone as my father began to break down again.

"You guys fought all of the time. It wasn't happiness. This was bound to happen at some point," I continued. It was bizarre to hear my father cry this much. But it felt liberating to finally tell my dad what I wanted to say instead of spending so much energy trying to avoid him and trying to protect myself from getting hurt by him again. I knew he was emotionally unstable. But I wondered if he was indirectly questioning my love for him.

"Dad, I have never really had a relationship with you. I have been very close to Mom my entire life. I always had a relationship with you through Mom. It would be great to have a relationship with you, just the two of us," I said.

I knew it wouldn't be appropriate to try to solve this huge emotional issue over the phone, so I quickly changed the subject. My father had told me the last time I saw him that he had joined a men's church group and I was curious to learn how it was.

"It is going really well," he said as he blew his nose into a tissue. "There are guys in the group that are divorced and some are remarried. It is nice to be around other guys who are going through what I am going through. We meet once a week at

Randy's house, where we read the scripture and apply the lessons to our lives," he said.

I had heard that Randy was a very conservative member of a much more conservative church than the Catholic church that we had attended when I was younger. Even though I was thankful that my father had a support group and an outlet to share what he was experiencing, I was concerned that my father was more vulnerable to the conservative teachings at this sensitive point in his life.

And I wondered just how far the group would probe. Now that he had been attending the weekly share group for a couple of months, I was sure that the group had naturally encouraged my father to share about his divorce experience. My mind spun through my dad's situation and could visualize how the questioning must have gone. Tell us about your family.

I can see my father pausing when it was time to bring me up. The bashful look on his face. The hesitation to divulge what he knew. The uncomfortable energy that must have radiated out of his being. How would he be able to even say the word gay out loud? Let alone say it to a conservative group of religious divorcees?

I had never told my father directly that I was gay. My mother had told him a couple years after I came out to her. And one summer after my mother told my father, I had brought up the topic of gay marriage on an early morning drive to an amusement park. I explained how I hoped that I could one day marry who I wanted to marry.

Even though my father only nodded during the conversation, I felt that my father had accepted me as gay. A sign of validation during the only time we ever talked about my sexuality.

And what if my father's acceptance had grown? What if he was now proud enough of me to declare my sexuality to a men's group from a church? Or would my father succumb to the group's reaction as he slowly told them? The thought made me snarl. I could visualize their eyes widening and noses scrunching in shock. The gasps as they exhaled in disgust. I had to know the truth.

"Well, it's ironic that you asked this question," my father calmly replied. "I have been wanting to chat with you about this topic for quite some time now, but I didn't know how to do it. And I have been praying to God for many weeks on how to discuss this with you. He must be listening to my prayers."

As my father threw out the God speak, it felt like an out-of-body experience. Like I was hovering over myself watching my reaction. I could feel my heart beat faster and became overwhelmed by a sense of excitement. I thought that I could finally talk about my sexuality with my father. That this could be the beginning of a strong bond between the two of us, something that I had always longed for.

"I've always felt this way but just didn't have any way to prove it," my father continued as I carefully listened. "But after the guys in the share group explained it to me about five or six times, it all makes sense," he said. My heart began to sink. The hopeful feelings I felt seconds earlier instantly eroded. My back and buttocks were now sweating against the leather seat in anticipation of what could possibly come out of his mouth next.

"This isn't your fault and I know it's not a choice that you had. But what was explained to me was that during conception, the devil somehow entered your body. And the devil has lived in your body since birth. The only way to rid the devil in your body is to accept Jesus Christ into your life. So there is good news. Once you read the Bible and accept its teachings, the devil will leave you and you will be free from what you are experiencing."

The dotted lines on the road in front of me sped by at 70 miles per hour as my head dropped forward and began shaking from side to side. My palms were now almost completely wet from sweat as they gripped the smooth leather steering wheel. *Did I just hear that from my father?*

"Wow, I guess if the devil entered me at conception, then either you or Mom is the devil," I sarcastically spewed out in disbelief. "I'm not really sure how the devil could just slip into the fertilization process."

I could only hear the hum of the engine. My father was on the line, but it was silent. I swallowed hard as my mouth became dry and my body went completely numb. How could my father believe this?

I began to explain to my father that the book he was reading and worshiping was written by human beings 2,000 to 3,000 years ago. Many analogies exist to this way of thinking. Like, I could write a book today that says drinking out of plastic bottles is a sin. Then over thousands of years with many re-writings and translation by human beings and some glorification along the way, the text becomes more powerful. And it becomes a sin to drink out of a plastic bottle.

Oh Leviticus, a book of the Bible that reflects a way of living life frozen in time. The all too common homosexuality and religion debate continued. I explained to him that it also says eating pork is an equal sin in the same book. And that the Bible also says my father can't get remarried since he was now divorced. That picking and choosing what you want to believe from the Bible is ignorant. But logic rarely works with this argument for people who are emotionally weak.

"Cory, this isn't your fault. This is something that has happened to you but only you can change," he explained. "I knew early on that you were different. But I didn't know what to do about it. Remember the brown teddy bear that you received when you had your tonsils out?"

My head slightly cocked to the side, trying to figure out where my father was going with the conversation. But even though the brown teddy bear took me back twenty-five years, I remembered it like it was yesterday.

BROWN TEDDY BEAR

MY THROAT BURNED as I sat up in the large hospital bed in my white gown recovering from surgery earlier that day. Only ice cream, shaved ice, and visitors bringing gifts would soothe the pain.

My father visited me later that evening after he finished working and handed me a large, wrapped gift that I proceeded to rip open. "Cool," I said as the large, remote control car appeared. I had to wait to play with it until we arrived home since I couldn't leave the bed, so we set it aside.

But I'll never forget unwrapping the super soft, brown teddy bear my godmother gave me. I smiled and hugged the bear hard. I knew I had a best friend for life. The bear's soft fur soothed me to sleep each night during my recovery. Years later, the teddy bear would become a memorable fixture as it sat on top of a bookshelf in our living room, reminding me of the comfort I felt during that scary time.

"This is the first time I noticed that you were different." My father choked up on his words over the phone. "It hurt me that you didn't want to play with the car but instead wanted to play with the teddy bear."

I could hear the years of distress in his voice. It shook me to know that my father had held onto this story for most of my life and never shared it with me until now. I began to wonder what other things he had been holding onto.

"Dad, you know me better than most other people. You watched me grow up. How can you really believe the devil is inside of me? Do you really need a group of guys who are very conservative to tell you this over and over until you believe it?" I lamented. I slowly began to realize that it didn't matter what I would say. My father's mind was already convinced that this was fact.

I began to plead with him. I wanted him to know that I have felt this in my being since I remember my first thoughts. That there was an attraction to boys instead of girls. And how I can't just flip a switch on my body somewhere to become straight. I was born this way. And that this isn't all me, but it is part of me.

"Believe me, Dad, growing up knowing that I may be gay has not been easy. I *knew* other people will hate me because I am not like them. Going through junior high and high school, I forced myself to act normal so I would fit in. So the bullying would stop," I continued.

"I was really afraid you would react this way. And it is why I have prayed about how to have this conversation with you. To let you know how I feel about it," he went on to say.

In an attempt to make him feel better, I explained that there wasn't anything that he did to make me gay. And there wasn't anything that my mother did. Some people are born with red hair. Some people are born with different skin colors. Some people have a disability. I was born gay. I didn't choose to be gay, and no one made me this way.

"Do you remember when you chose to be straight? That one day you had a girl and a boy in front of you and you just chose the girl?" I asked.

"Well, no," he answered.

"Exactly. You didn't choose your sexuality. Just like I didn't choose my sexuality. It works the same for everyone. We were made perfectly. We were born exactly the way God intended."

CATHOLIC GUILT

MY ENTIRE BODY shook from telling my father how I felt after it was clear he believed I was going to hell. Years of tightly sealed emotions rattled through my internal wiring and up through my brain. The confined energy triggered memories I hadn't processed in a long time. Uncomfortable childhood memories bubbled up, reminding me of the guilt and shame I lived each day. It took me back to the seventh grade.

I was excited to have a day off from school, but I wasn't excited to attend the local Catholic church's day-long educational service for all of the children of Catholic faith from the sixth to the eighth grade.

A man in his seventies wearing a long white robe and a tall, pointed white hat stood in front of the boys seated on the ground in the large assembly hall connected to the church next door, where all the girls had been ushered into. The priest encouraged us to write down any type of question that we had about religion and place it into a bowl that was being passed around so the question would remain anonymous as it was read aloud. The bowl was handed to me and I threw in a blank piece of paper since I had no clue what to ask. I looked around and saw most of my classmates doing the same thing.

The priest sat down in a wooden chair at the front as all the boys intently watched his moves wondering what would happen next. He proceeded to pull out white slips of paper and all of us looked around smiling at each other thinking he would find a bunch of blank pieces of paper.

"Is it a sin to masturbate?" he read off of the first paper with a question on it. In an instant, the room fell eerily still. My eyebrows raised, wondering who would be brave enough to write that question. In perfect choreography, the priest stood up and slowly began walking around the seated group in a large circle. As he walked around us, his hands were raised up to his chest and his fingertips lightly touched each other. His wide-open eyes were fixated straight ahead like a zombie in some sort of trance.

Our eyes collectively followed him around our circle as our bodies remained still, like we would be punished if we moved. Our ears intently listened to his monotone voice explaining how it was a sin to touch yourself.

I was too scared to giggle. My stomach twisted as I slowly swallowed, trying to realize what was happening. The priest came back around to the front. We could all hear the small pieces of paper mix around as he swirled his hand around in the glass bowl. I strained my eyes to see if I could see anything written on the paper as he pulled out another small white piece.

"Is homosexuality a sin?" his aged, raspy voice produced. Some of the boys close by giggled as he spoke. I was confused and could feel my heart beating faster. I had heard this word before, but didn't know exactly what it meant.

The white-robed zombie began to slowly walk around the group again, but this time in the other direction. As the priest explained homosexuality, "gay" and "if two boys liked each other more than friends and they kissed," the faces on all of the boys shriveled up.

"Ewwwww."

"Gross."

I could see the corner of the priest's lips begin to raise up and his eyes slightly narrow as his towering figure slowly began surveying the group of boys sitting cross-legged below. My breathing sped up. I looked up thinking that at any moment lightning would pierce through the roof above and strike me.

I was terrified that the priest would see into my soul and know my thoughts. I looked around at my classmates to see if they noticed how uncomfortable I was. But no one could see the guilt that bubbled inside of me. My body remained motionless the rest of the question-and-answer period as my mind shut down in fear.

When I arrived home later that afternoon, I shut myself in my room before anyone could see me. Tears began to roll down my face as I pulled out a piece of origami paper. I picked up a pen and my hand shook as I wrote.

"Cory, You will not like boys anymore. You are not gay. Being gay is a sin and you will go to hell for eternity. Love, Cory"

I carefully folded the piece of paper into the shape of a heart and looked around my room for places to hide my note where no one would find it. I stood up on a chair to reach a small, brown chest with a small latch that sat on a shelf along the wall across from my bed. Inside the chest was a collection of cassette tapes that I no longer listened to. I opened the case for the single, "Final Countdown" by Europe, stuffed my note between the inside cover and the actual cassette tape, and buried the closed case at the bottom of the chest.

I put the chest back up on the shelf and felt a sense of relief wash over me. God could now see that I would not sin anymore. I placed the chair back at my desk and looked back up at the shelf. I took a deep breath and raised my hands to wipe away my tears.

Several days later, an episode of 'Saved by the Bell' was playing on the television in the living room as I was folding laundry. After I folded everything out in the living room, I grabbed piles to distribute everything where it belonged.

I walked down the hallway and hesitated before entering my sister's room. I took a deep breath and turned through her door. My knees went weak every time my eyes met the poster of Patrick Swayze staring down at me with his shirt off from above my sister's bed. I could feel my body heat up with excitement as I stood transfixed with my sister's socks in my hand.

My body was still buzzing with excitement after I put all the folded laundry away. I crept down the hallway and into my bedroom, quietly closing the door behind me. I felt the soft cushion below my feet as I stood on my chair to pull down the brown chest on the shelf. After pulling out the cassettes, I found the note that I had written days earlier.

I unwrapped the heart-shaped note to unveil the promise that I had made to myself. My head began to shake as I stared down at the words. The energy in my soul overpowered my brain and my hands pulled the note in opposite directions. I could hear the paper tearing down the center. In seconds, the promise and my guilt had been shredded into small pieces so no one could ever put it back together.

The pressure had released from my mind. For a moment, the guilt lifted away. My body collapsed into my bed still buzzing with excitement. I was now free to explore without holding back. And explore my sexuality without judging myself.

But after my release, guilt quickly took over my mind and my body. I feared that I had sinned again. The image of the priest popped back into my mind. I saw his lips widen and his eyes closely watching his fearful students below. I was shaking.

I reached for a piece of paper and wrote the same note to myself. I folded up the paper and hid the note again in the same place.

This ritual continued into high school. The guilt would pulse through my body knowing that I may go to hell one day for all of the sins I committed. I felt alone. I felt like an outcast. I wasn't normal.

My guilt would be exacerbated at school by the jeers from my classmates. The other boys would call me a girl because most of my friends were girls. But I hung my head low, knowing I wasn't one of the popular kids. I was in band and choir while all the jocks in the school played sports, just as my father had.

I tried so hard to fit in every day. I wanted to make sure I hid these dark feelings I harbored. No one could find out. I learned at an early age that I had to somehow act the way others wanted me to act. That I couldn't be myself or it would be forced suicide. I feared that someone in my small town would find out about my secret.

The exhaustion from hiding became too much for me to handle at times. Some days at an early age, I felt it would just be easier not being here at all. If I ended my life. That is what all the "normal" people wanted. Society wanted me to fit in. And I knew I didn't fit in.

As I recounted the fear and shame and wanting to fit in at an early age in my mind, I remembered that I was still having a conversation with my father.

I jumped into the silence. "I'm struggling with where to go from here. I know that you are going through a very tough time in your life right now. And I want you to be happy. I know you joined this group and they are helping you in many ways overcome your sadness. But I can't accept what you are telling me. You are asking me to be someone I am not. You want me to be someone like you. I think that is what you have always wanted me to be. But I am not. I am who I am. This is how I was born. I guess maybe we will just have to agree to disagree with this situation." I didn't really know what else to say.

"I guess we'll just agree to disagree. I still love you, Cory. And I pray for you every night. I have a picture of you next to my bed and I pray that you can accept Jesus Christ and be happy," my father said.

"I'm arriving at my condo. Goodbye, Dad," I said. I was ready to end this life-changing call.

"God bless you, Cory" my father said as he hung up the phone. I pulled into the covered parking structure of my condo building, shut my car off, and sat in silence. I looked ahead, dazed. The pit of my stomach knotted up. I quickly leaned out of the car door and dry heaved toward the black pavement. Nothing came out of my mouth except shock.

GRANDMA OF CONVERSION THERAPY

MY T-SHIRT STUCK to my wet skin as I jumped up from a deep sleep in the queen-sized bed centered in my hotel room. My hands touched the damp sheet where I had been lying while my eyes adjusted to the dark, unfamiliar space. Just moments earlier, my father appeared through the doorway. I saw his evil grin and his bright red eyes staring at me. His head tilted backward and his mouth opened, producing a deep, haunting laugh.

He licked his wet, red lips and began to creep toward me. His hairy arms were outstretched and his claw-like fingers curled forward. I was paralyzed with fear as he approached. He let out an unfathomable roar as thick saliva drooped out of each side of his mouth. As he launched toward me, I let out a scream and jumped up.

Once my heartbeat returned back to normal, I lay back down and shut my eyes, trying to get some more sleep before my weekend MBA class began in a few hours.

My phone's loud, buzzing alarm switched on as planned and my exhausted body twitched. I rubbed my sleepy eyes with my clammy hands. My arms reached up into the stale air, trying to jumpstart my cloudy mind.

I sat at the edge of the bed staring at the bright sunlight forcing its way into the room from the sides of the thick window shade. I had become an expert at blocking things out of my mind for years, so I thought blocking out nightmares about my father would be no different.

Several weeks later, midway through a flight back to Florida from a weeklong business trip in Portland, Oregon, I dozed off in my window seat, which was rare because I have trouble sleeping while sitting upright on flights.

I heard terrifying screams and saw people fly out of their seats as the plane began to nosedive. I looked out the window and saw my father seated on the wing of the plane. He turned his head, revealing his bright red eyes. He clenched his teeth together and let out a growl that vibrated through his throat. My jaw dropped open and my eyes widened. The plane sped up in complete freefall. The ground quickly approached and I braced my arms around my head, preparing for my fate.

My head jerked backward and my clenched hands popped up, grabbing the seat in front me. The elderly woman next to me quickly shook away from me as my body jolted. I turned my head to look outside and saw the motionless wing gliding through the air. All seemed to be ok.

"I'm so sorry," I quietly said to the woman beside me as she held her hands over her chest, trying to catch her breath. I exhaled, knowing that I was ok. But I also knew this recurring nightmare wasn't going to go away. It was probably time to speak with someone about what I was going through to help me deal with my feelings.

It made me anxious to think about finding a therapist I could connect with. I didn't have time to ask around for recommendations, so I called up the third-party organization who managed my employer's Employee Assistance Program and asked for a list of experienced, LGBT-friendly therapists near my home. The woman I eventually chose had over 50 years of experience. I was positive she would be able to validate the feelings that I was experiencing and help guide me out of this tough life moment.

Even though I was no stranger to therapy, my nerves gripped my stomach as I drove to my first therapy session. A feeling of uneasiness overcame me as I pulled into a parking lot behind a church. I looked again at the therapist's address and then again at my GPS to make sure I was in the right place. Everything was correct. My stomach began to turn over.

Even though I was ten minutes early, I climbed the rusty, maroon-colored metal stairs on the back side of the church. The area under my arms of my collared, button-down blue shirt began to turn a darker shade as my body heated up. I pulled the metal door open and walked into the fluorescent lighting of the small entryway that led into a larger community space.

Only half of the long tube lights on the ceiling were illuminated and I wasn't quite sure if I was in the right place since it was the common area of the church. It wasn't your typical therapist's office.

"Hello," I said, hoping someone would hear me. But the wooden paneling on the walls deadened my voice. It was eerily quiet for a Wednesday evening at a church. I sat down on one of the orange-cushioned wooden chairs positioned on the white tiled floor along the wall.

Not long after I sat down, I had this feeling that I was in the wrong location, so I got up and began to walk around. Across the open room I noticed a wooden door with a long narrow vertical window embedded on one side. A small placard next to the door listed my therapist's name. I peered inside the window and saw a small woman with white hair wrapped in a bun on top of her head seated motionless in a wooden rocking chair facing away from the door.

I slowly turned the door handle, pulled the door open a little, and softly said, "Dr. Friedman?"

The woman's body flinched and began to rock attempting to rise out of the chair. "Yes," she said with a soft, almost childlike voice.

I walked into the room and up to Dr. Friedman. My mouth was dry and nervous energy festered under my skin. Still seated, she reached out her frail hand to grab my extended arm as a friendly greeting. I sat down on a worn, plaid couch about ten feet away from her chair, positioned in front of the only window in the concrete block room.

"Tell me why you are here," she started, without much introduction. Her smile pulled back the wrinkled skin on her cheeks as the red strap from the thick glasses that dominated her face drooped down on each side of her head.

"I wanted to have an initial meeting with you. I am trying to find a therapist in the area that I can work with to help me overcome some difficult emotions that I have been experiencing as a result of a conversation I had with my father earlier this year," I replied. "And I want to find someone who has experience dealing with LGBT family situations. I saw that you had been a therapist for quite some time and may have dealt with similar situations in the past."

There was a long pause but no reaction from her. Not even an expression change. A few awkward moments passed as I quickly glanced around the room at all the images of Jesus and Mary staring down at me.

"Tell me more about this conversation that you had with your father," she slowly replied after what seemed like several minutes of silence.

I recounted the disturbing dialogue my father and I had exchanged and how I was still in shock, trying to figure out what I should do. As I shared the story, my chest trembled with deep emotions that bubbled up inside of me. We discussed more about the relationship I had with my father over the course of the past

30 years of my life, but my uneasy feeling about this therapist continued to build. She began to ask me questions about my sexuality and when I had begun having thoughts about being gay.

During an awkward moment, she abruptly said that our time had ended. As I sat feeling very confused, I watched as she rocked herself out of the chair and stood up with all of her energy. She slowly walked into a small room in the far corner and after several minutes came back out holding a thin book.

"I want you to go through this workbook on emotions and begin it before our next session," she said as she handed me the floppy book. "You will need to pay me ten dollars later for the workbook, but you can have it now." I felt slightly relieved knowing that I had some homework. I knew it was a way for me to think deeper about my feelings and potentially help me.

However, I couldn't stop thinking about Dr. Friedman's strange questioning during my ten-minute drive home as the sun was setting. It didn't feel quite right in my gut. After I finished dinner that evening, I was eager to get started on my emotional recovery. I pulled out the workbook and sat down at my kitchen table with a pen, excited to jump in.

As I began reading the first exercise, I shook my head in disbelief. I flipped through the rest of the workbook and couldn't believe my eyes. This wasn't any normal workbook for clients trying to overcome difficult family situations like mine. Instead, this was a workbook used for conversion therapy programs—religious programs sponsored by conservative churches attempting to make homosexual people heterosexual.

My heart sank as I flipped the workbook closed. I walked out onto my balcony and into the warm evening air, placed both of my hands on the metal railing, and stared down at the pool lined with lush, tropical landscaping within the brightly lit courtyard. I gently closed my eyes as I slowly exhaled and tried to calm myself down.

The workbook remained untouched on my kitchen table for days. Each time I walked by, I hoped an answer would pop up about what I should do with it, but my mind went blank. I felt helpless.

The following Wednesday after work, I drove back to Dr. Friedman's office for our next scheduled appointment. I parked my car in the same spot as last week, but this time I felt anger instead of anxiety. Earlier that day, my blood boiled when I wrote a letter explaining my disappointment with her services and explained that I was recommending to my Employee Assistance Program that she be removed from their roster of available therapists.

A strong breeze blew the humid evening air into my car when I opened the door. Dark storm clouds loomed on the horizon, juxtaposing the blue sky overhead. With the workbook and letter firmly in my hand, I confidently walked up the worn metal stairs and into the church. My jaw firmly squeezed together as I walked across the open area to Dr. Friedman's office.

Without hesitation, I pulled open the closed door to her office and saw her seated in the same position that I found her in last week. With a faux-warm expression on my face, I held out the book and the letter.

She looked up at me in hesitation since I did not continue onto the couch. In a polite tone, I explained that I was returning her unused workbook and that I would no longer meet with her. The wrinkles on her forehead pulled down with a look of confusion.

I held my lips tightly together, turned toward the open door, and felt a calm presence wrap around me as I slowly walked out of the building. Once the door closed behind me, I stood looking out over the two cars in the parking lot below. I could feel adrenaline pumping through my veins that had built up over the past week.

The dark clouds had drifted overhead and began to block out the setting sunlight. My chest pumped up as I took a huge breath. After holding onto my breath for a couple seconds, I slowly emptied the air, releasing the tension I had been holding within my shoulders.

I sat down in my car as the sky darkened further. Cool air blew from the vent as my mind raced back to how this entire situation with my father began over six months ago.

As I put my car into drive, I looked up and saw Dr. Friedman carefully open the exterior door to the church and step onto the stairway. She locked the church door and grabbed the railing, guiding her seventy-something-year-old body down the stairs. And as she slowly descended the stairs, the black sky opened up.

A powerful, drenching rain emptied out of the dark clouds. I couldn't help but watch in amazement as the heavens performed justice. Dr. Friedman was instantly soaked as she struggled to continue down the slippery metal stairs.

God had opened up his power. Powerful thunder rattled the area as the rain continued to dump down. God clearly sent a message that he loves all his children and that all humans were created equally—as they are.

Dr. Friedman's white hair fell down the side of her drenched face in a ratted clump. Her thick glasses had steamed over and dark streaks formed under her eyes as the rain eroded her heavy eye makeup. I wanted to make sure she safely made it to her car, but a great sense of relief filled my soul. My smile widened and I knew that I would be just fine.

2
I'M NOT MY FATHER'S SON

LOLA

S EVEN YEARS LATER, after moving back to New York, I sat in the dark Broadway theater next to my good friend Leah, who was visiting me for the weekend from Florida. She wanted to see a Broadway show while she was visiting New York City.

Leah was a tough girl and rarely showed any sign of emotion. She was an extremely loyal friend who protected everyone she cared deeply about. A Florida girl through and through, Leah was in her happy spot when she was in her bikini out in the sun with a mimosa in her hand. Her straight, bleach-blonde hair came down to her shoulders and when she threw on a pair of high heels, our eyes were at the same level.

I didn't know which shows were available last minute, but as I was browsing through the list, Kinky Boots popped up and I remembered how much fun this musical was. Leah had always wanted to see the show, so it was perfect.

The main supporting character, Lola, had paused on stage before easing into a song in the middle of the first act. It was a moment in the musical where Lola, a male character, was eloquently describing his experience of becoming a drag queen in spite of his father not agreeing.

His voice was soft and pure. The entire theater became still. No one moved and every eyeball was held in suspense to hear what was going to come next. Goosebumps ran up my legs and arms and up through my neck. I closed my eyes as my ears absorbed the sweet notes.

A lump developed in my throat as the sound from the orchestra below reached the upper deck and began to envelop my body. I had seen this musical once before, but I had forgotten about this song. The emotional words harmoniously flowed from Lola's mouth sharing how his father avoided seeing the best part of him.

IN THE WEEDS

AS I HELD my eyes closed, I began to see my small, thin childhood frame floating in the water next to my father's old speedboat out on the lake in front of my parents' lake house. They had purchased the land when my sister and I were toddlers and eventually built a house that would become our family's summer weekend getaway. It was the late 1980s which meant we had no cell phone service and my parents had not installed a landline, so it was a perfect escape from the busy lives we all had.

My father was an electrician by trade and worked very hard to buy the things that he did. I was about ten years old when my dad bought a very used early-1980s Glastron inboard motorboat. He also bought some water tubes to pull behind the boat. My father would pull my sister and I around the lake on the tubes, spinning us before we would fall off. The excitement of going fast out on the open water on the tube was exhilarating.

The lake wasn't a large lake and my family's property was at the southern tip where it narrowed and became shallow. Unfortunately, in the springtime, weeds would quickly grow in front of our property and fill the shallow area since the rays of sun easily reached the bottom. Often, other boats would come into our area of the lake, but would have to stop because the motor would become overwhelmed by the thick weeds.

It was one of those days in early summer where the temperature was unseasonably hot. Not a cloud graced the perfectly blue sky. The green leaves on the trees were brand new and breathing in the clean country air. My mom, sister, dad, and I wanted to get out on the water to cool down to take advantage of the lake.

We pushed back from the white-painted wooden dock and my dad began to slowly navigate through the weedy lake jungle. My dad struggled to turn the steering wheel each way since the power steering wasn't that great. It was one of the drawbacks to owning an antique. After a short while, you could visibly see his frustration of having to expend so much energy to enjoy the day. I always wondered if he was just frustrated he was stuck with the old boat, or if he knew that he had no control over the weeds that sprouted basically overnight.

He managed to maneuver the boat about fifty yards out from the dock toward the large, open non-weedy water in front of us. We could see other boats freely zipping along the relatively calm waters. We only had about twenty yards left until we were free from the thick foliage holding us temporarily hostage. Just when we thought we found our way out of the maze, the noise from the motor quickly changed to a much higher pitch and my father instantly shut off the boat.

Sweat dripped from my father's forehead as he worked hard to find a clear path out of the weeds. While he raised his forearm to wipe away the sweat, his jaw clenched together hard and his face turned bright red with anger. He walked to the back of the boat and peered over the edge down at the water.

As he leaned over, his head fell forward quickly as he exhaled. My mom, sister, and I all knew what had happened, but experience taught us not to say anything to him at this point because he would blast out at us in anger from his frustration.

At ten years old, I certainly did not exude power. I was the opposite of power. My frame was small and you could see my rib bones protruding my skin when I had my shirt off.

As the bright sun hit our skin while we sat in the boat in the weeds, I wondered what was going to happen next. We all expected my dad to jump into the water and go under the boat to pull the weeds out. I've seen him do it before and it didn't look fun. My dad would have to go under water many times and reach with his arms to pull the long, vine-like weeds out of the intake grate. He couldn't wear a life jacket because it would prevent him from going underwater to reach the area he needed to clear.

And while trying to pull out the weeds from the intake grate, he also needed to battle the thick vegetation floating in the water. Navigating the lake at that point was like floating in a thick pudding of weeds.

I looked back at our lake house, thinking maybe this wasn't a great idea.

"Ok, Cory, jump in and clean out the weeds," my father said in an annoyed tone, looking away as he motioned out toward the water, indicating I needed to get in. My head snapped around to send him a confused look. My dad sometimes joked around, so I was trying to get a sign from him that he was kidding.

"Al, Cory is too small to do that. It's dangerous," my mother said. She knew my father wasn't joking.

"No, Cory is going to do this," he replied in a stern voice to assert his control.

"Why can't you jump in and do this like you have before?" my mom hesitantly responded.

"Cory can do it," he said defiantly as he turned around from the back of the boat, shooting a piercing look at her and me.

Fear immediately raced through me. It wasn't only fear of swimming under the boat amidst all of the weeds in the water, but it was fear of my dad. Fear of what would happen if I said no. Fear of the consequences of standing up to him.

At the time, I didn't quite know if he wanted to show his power or if he wanted to toughen me up. My father could see that I was not as physically tough as he was. He feared having a son that appeared physically weak.

"No, I don't want to do this," I said. My voice quivered. My father must have noticed my body recoil as he looked at me.

"Cory, we aren't going anywhere until you clean out the weeds," my father said in an aggressive tone as my sister and mother helplessly looked on.

I quickly looked over at my mother for help. I could tell she wanted to come to my defense and save me as she had many times in the past. But she knew saving me would have further consequences for her. She was constantly playing the game of choosing which battle to fight and which one not to fight, as my dad never knew how to lose an argument.

"Go on." He grunted as he pointed at the water.

I looked into my mother's eyes as I felt warm tears roll down my face, realizing I was not going to get out of this. I turned away from everyone to hide the terrified look on my face. As I closed my eyes hoping to escape this moment, I imagined a giant bird swooping down and taking a massive dump on my dad. He would be forced to get into the water to clean off and then clean out the weeds so I didn't have to.

My lungs tried to pull in air as my tears became uncontrollable. I didn't know how I was going to go underwater and tug at the weeds that were jammed up into the grate with my thin arms. The task seemed too dangerous for someone my size.

But I knew I didn't have a choice. I would be forced to if I refused. I turned around. My dad stared at me with a controlling and unforgiving look. Like a bully would stare at their next victim. My mom sat helplessly as her eyes moistened. This carefree day began so beautifully but was becoming a day that I will sadly remember for the rest of my life.

I wiped away the tears from my face with both hands and stood up on the vinyl seat along the side of the boat. I put my hands on the boat's side and peered over into what looked like a giant mound of green spaghetti floating in brown soup.

I stepped over the edge and sat my buttocks on the side of the boat. I raised my head out toward the lake to see if anyone was watching what was happening. Like I was hoping for the child police to swiftly come over and halt what was about to happen. I raised my body with my hands on the edges and pushed off.

My light body slid into the spaghetti soup below. Slimy foliage tickled my feet as I initially touched the water, then the sliminess surrounded my entire body once my head went under.

My mom and sister stood up and leaned over the side to make sure I was ok while my dad just stood at the back of the boat waiting until the deed was done. The weeds were thick all the way down. I pulled my arms backward at my sides to push myself to the side of the boat.

With a quick glance upward at my mom and sister to let them know I was ok, I took a huge breath, closed my eyes and sunk under the water. I could feel the bottom of the boat with my arm as I slowly moved closer to the grate. My eyes remained shut, as

I wouldn't be able to see anything with the weeds pushing up against my face.

I moved my hands around for a couple seconds, but I couldn't feel anything besides the boat's smooth bottom. The pressure of holding the air in my lungs began to make my heart beat faster. It felt like I was running out of air, so I decided to turn around to go back out to where I began.

I began to pull myself back out. My arms moved around faster as I felt the bottom of the boat, but didn't remember going this far underneath. The fiberglass bottom had grooves that ran from front to back, so I knew I was going toward the side as I felt them moving in a perpendicular direction.

Kick. Kick. Kick. My legs did a lot of work without really going anywhere as the weeds didn't allow for much propulsion. In fact, the long weeds had tangled around me.

My small hands tried gripping the fiberglass groove to try to pull myself. I had to use my arms to pull with all of my might, but my fingers just slipped off the groove. My heart raced and took away my breath faster than it should. I kicked my legs in different directions like a frog kick and coordinated my arm pulls at the same time to try to force myself forward.

Using the very last amount of energy my frail body had saved, my arms and legs kicked hard in unison and my head came out of the water. I opened my mouth and gasped for new oxygen to enter my empty lungs. I wiped the water from my eyes as my legs kicked to stay afloat.

"Are you ok?" my mom asked as she peered over the edge of the boat. My lungs continued to quickly pull in air. She reached behind her and then dropped a life jacket down to me since she could see me struggling. I shivered with fear.

"Calm down, it's ok." My mom encouraged me to stay strong. "Did you get the weeds out?"

She had no clue how bad it was. I shook my head from side to side as my breathing was still trying to catch up. I didn't want to alarm her that it was going to take many trips for me to pull out all the weeds that were jammed up into the grate.

As I held onto the life jacket with my legs dangling among the weed soup, I felt weak and small. I was unable to even reach the grate to pull any weeds out on my first attempt. What would my father think? What if I didn't come back out from under the boat with my next try? Maybe that was how the universe wanted my time to end? Maybe that would be a life lesson for my dad if I didn't make it out.

My heartbeat returned to a more normal pace. As I waited for my breathing to calm down, I continued staring back across the lake toward our lake house and I became angry. I became angry that my dad was forcing me to do this. My dad wanted me to be strong. He wanted me to be tough like him. Unfortunately, these attempts at toughening me up only made me fear him. The situations pushed me away from him.

Now I wanted to prove that I was not weak. I wanted to prove that I could do this. But it wasn't to prove to him. It was to prove to me. Courage grew through my entire being. I could do this. I would win—for me.

Without looking back toward my mom, I took a huge breath and pulled myself under the water. On this attempt I reached the grate quicker. The entire intake area was plugged with the thick weeds. I reached my hand out to grab onto a handful and tried to tug. The weeds were tightly jammed into the grate. I needed leverage to pull the weeds loose, but I had nothing to push against or hold onto.

Managing my breath and energy better this time, I was able to position myself directly under the center of the boat. The rectangular intake area consisted of eight thick metal rods three feet long spread about three inches apart. I managed to maneuver my fingers to grip my left hand around one of the rods while using my right hand to clench small portions of the weeds.

The weeds were slimy and my hand had trouble holding on as I pulled. After several tries of not being able to pull anything out, I opened up my hand like a small claw, reached into the thick bundle between two of the rods and then closed my claw-like hand around the weeds. Holding onto the rod above as leverage with my other hand, I used all of my might to pull the large clump. The weeds shifted and slowly began to come out.

I knew that I only needed to get a small portion dislodged to create space, then the other weeds would come out easier. The compression in my chest and throat began to worsen. I had used up a lot of energy and needed to get out. I turned my body so my chest and face were almost touching the bottom of the boat. I gripped my feet on one of the grate rods and pushed as hard as I could with my legs. This time the momentum carried me quickly to the side of the boat and my head popped up out of the water.

As new air pulled quickly into my lungs, I smiled a little, knowing that I was on my way to conquering this situation. Once I caught my breath again, I went back under the boat and continued to pull big heaps of weeds out each time. Three more courageous trips and I had done it.

I swam around to the back of the boat and I pulled myself up the small ladder that was flipped down. My mother wrapped a towel around me. And with a proud smile on her face, she wrapped her loving arms around me, too. She had always been my hero. But that day, I think I was her hero.

THE FINAL GOODBYE

THE SWEET SOUND kissed my ears and I opened my eyes back to the motionless theater. My jaw clenched as I tried to hold back tears. But they were inevitable. My lips pressed tightly together as the drops of water rolled down my warm cheeks. Tears from my past that had been held in time, waiting for the right moment to be released as I listened to the heartfelt words of the song. Lola explained how he wasn't his father's son. How his father had created an image of Lola in his mind that wasn't who Lola truly was.

I could sense myself trying to hold back the floodgates. People would see me cry and I would be a mess. Crying in public is not something we see very often, so when it happens, it becomes a moment, something almost unacceptable. Even at the theater, in this moment, my mind wanted to hold back for fear of what others would see and think.

But I let go. I let go of holding back. I let go of worrying. I hung my head down and my body shook in a hard cry. My hands were clenched together on my lap as the music fanned me with love. Leah reached over and grabbed my hand. She squeezed it tightly, sending her love through her soul and into mine.

I felt a warm hand from behind me gently lay on my left shoulder. And in that moment, I could feel the words entering my mind, "You are loved. You are the person you were meant to be. You are enough." The person behind me was an angel. I was surrounded by love.

CLOSING MY EYES, my mind drifted back seven years to when I had lived in Florida. Weeks after my run-in with the grandma of conversion therapy, my search for meaning followed a new path when I located a new therapist who accepted me as me. Barb greeted me at the front door of a house that had been converted into a therapy practice. I noticed her limp immediately as I followed her back to her office. One of her legs was longer than the other and she had to wear special shoes to compensate for the difference.

Barb's long brown curly hair swung over to one side as she sat down in her chair behind her desk. I positioned myself in the soft, faux leather chair situated directly in front of her desk. I noticed a bathroom off to the side of the room, which was once part of the master suite that was now her office.

As I drove to her office each Wednesday after work, I anticipated the insights that I would walk away with after our conversations. Barb's gentle voice by itself was therapeutic, but I could feel deep in my heart that I was on my way to a life unlock. She would challenge me by throwing out thought-provoking questions during key moments of our conversation to help me dig deeper into areas that I may be covering up as a protection mechanism.

Barb could see the hurt and emotional pain on my face as I looked down at my clasped hands in my lap with disappointment. Birds outside the window sang their evening song as I sat in silence with Barb looking on with an empathetic gaze.

I looked up at the ceiling to hold back my tears and pictured my future husband and potential children meeting my father one day. I thought about how awkward it would be for my partner and I to be with my father knowing that he would be envisioning red horns on top of our heads with red tails coming from behind us.

"Have you ever thought about writing a letter to your father?" Barb suggested toward the end of our emotional session. "More as a way to communicate to him instead of having another painful conversation with him."

"I have thought about that. But I don't quite know what to say," I responded, knowing that trying to change my father's mind was worthless. "Continuing dialogue with someone that has their mind made up is not worth the time and emotional energy. I don't want to continue going through the same pain I am going through now."

"Your father's mind is made up," she continued as I slowly nodded my head. "But this letter wouldn't be an attempt to try to convince him of anything. It would be a way to share your truth. To share the principles that you live by as an adult.

"We are born to parents that we don't choose. While biological parents will always be your biological parents, there is no steadfast law that states we must have a close relationship with them. And a loving, emotional relationship doesn't exist between two people if one person can't accept all of the other's authentic qualities. All of them and not just some of them.

"If your father doesn't accept you for all the greatness that you are—including your sexuality, which is a unique part of your greatness—then why is it an imperative that you continue having a relationship with him? Especially if it will cause you further hurt and pain? This letter would be your way of telling him you no longer can have a relationship with someone that can't accept all of you.

"You always have the option of not sending the letter. This is mainly to help you."

I sat in deep thought for a moment. After growing up in a loving and close-knit family full of memorable holiday and birthday celebrations with my cousins and aunts and uncles on both sides of my family, the concept of releasing a relationship with my father seemed unimaginable.

As she watched my brain turn over, she slowly proceeded in a soft tone, "I want you to consider two things. What if your father does not ever respond to your letter? And if your father passed away today, would you have any regrets?"

My eyes welled up as I knew in my gut that my relationship with my father had already died. I wasn't the boy he had hoped for. The son he always wanted. And now the Church had taken his ability to follow his own gut. To know what is right and what is wrong for himself.

I walked out of my therapist's office that day with more clarity than I ever had about my father. Without hesitation, I drove to Target and walked into the card section. Hundreds of cards positioned in the nicely organized rows lined the aisle. I thought the sympathy section may have a card that would say something to the effect of what I wanted to convey.

"With sympathy..." I put the card back, not feeling that was the appropriate tone. I moved over to another aisle and found the Papyrus section. Fun images of dogs and beach scenes and flowers all sat in nice plastic covers. The card had to be simple. I leaned down to look at some other options of blank cards.

I reached out and picked up a card that had an image of a golden sunset at a beach. I turned it over to see if there was a message inside, but the card was perfectly blank. I bought the card.

Once home, I took out a piece of notebook paper and began to write. "There is no switch to flip." "I was born this way." "You are being brainwashed."

I continued writing different ideas and thoughts that I wanted to convey to my father as I sat on my couch after making some dinner. But I didn't want to accuse or be negative. My message had to be simple and direct. I became frustrated and I ended up scratching off most everything I wrote. I decided I will just sleep on it since there was no rush.

My eyes flipped open from a deep sleep. I sat up in bed, "That's it!" I said out loud. As I pulled the covers off of me and stepped out of bed, the red numbers in my alarm clock read 3:18 am. The light from the courtyard below filtered into my room, which gave me enough light to find my way to the kitchen where I had left the piece of paper.

> *"Dad,*
> *Until you can accept me for the person God created*
> *me to be,*
> *I can no longer have a relationship with you.*
> *God Bless,*
> *Cory"*

As I passed by the kitchen counter the next morning, I was ready. I looked down at the paper and took a large deep breath. The importance of the moment felt like I was signing important legal documents. Years of emotional baggage expelled through 26 words. Tightly gripping the sealed envelope between my fingers, I walked out of my apartment and hopped into my car.

It was one of those perfect Florida spring mornings with no clouds in the sky. The warm air flowed through the window as I drove to the post office. My Cadillac slowly came to stop and I reached over to pick up the card that sat alone in the passenger seat. As I gripped the edges with both hands and gazed down at the front of the white envelope, I felt no fear. I felt no doubt. I pulled the card to my lips and kissed my father's hand-written name, thinking maybe one day he would wake up from this religion-induced coma.

My eyes followed the card as I released it and it disappeared into the mail slot alongside the red brick post office. With a couple blinks of my eyes, I turned away, put on my sunglasses, and slowly drove off. The air that entered my nose felt purer than it had before. The tension in my back and shoulders had relaxed. I had released my father from the memories of the internal pain that he had unknowingly created. My soul became lighter as the chapter ended.

The following month, I pulled into my assigned parking space under my condo building after a long day of work and passed by the mail room before heading up to my apartment. I pulled out the small stack of mail that was grouped together in my mailbox and proceeded up the elevator to the fourth floor. As the elevator door closed, I flipped through the envelopes quickly, seeing mostly junk mail. But then I stopped at the second-to-last envelope—one that was addressed to me in distinct handwriting.

I thought it was strange that my father had sent me a card. The humidity inside of the elevator had moistened my hands as I pulled my finger through the top edge of the envelope and pulled out a card with a green generic design. Curiosity struck me as I flipped the card open. My father's slanted left-handed writing filled the entire white space in perfectly positioned rows of cursive text.

The elevator door opened and I slowly stepped out while reading the card. As I walked down the hallway to my unit, I looked up and paused. I was surprised to think that I had forgotten about sending my father a card last month and now he was responding.

My father explained that he loves me very much and wanted to have a relationship with me. But he explained that he could not change his thoughts about my sexuality. That he believes in the power of the Bible and Jesus Christ. And that maybe this situation was something that we could agree to disagree about.

"Agree to disagree?" I yelled out loud, standing in front of my door. My eyes rolled back into my head and I unlocked my door to go inside. I set my computer bag down on my dining room table and reread the card for a second time in utter disbelief.

We could disagree on what our favorite color was or what our favorite city was. Or what food tasted better. Or even if holding hands in public was acceptable or not. We could certainly agree to disagree. But this was my life. This was my soul. This was who I was born to be.

I flipped the card shut. My scab had been picked open. My hands gripped the top of the card and pulled in opposite directions. The card split in two. I pulled those pieces into more pieces. My foot pushed down on the pedal at the base of the trash can, flipping open the lid. As the pieces dropped into the black bag below, I knew it was over.

THE HOUSE LIGHTS came on as we finished clapping for the incredible cast. Leah and I turned toward each other and she saw my red eyes as I wiped away the residual tears from the show. She leaned in and gave me a big embrace, which I know was not easy for her to do in public. But in that moment, she knew I needed her.

3
100% BELIEVABLE BUT ONLY 95% TRUE

DISAPPEARING ACT

"WHERE HAVE YOU been?" my new friend Sarah asked with a puzzled look on her face when I walked into the dormitory lobby, taking my coat off. "I have been really worried about you." She was sitting next to my roommate and they both stood up out of the soft, cushioned chairs like they had been anxiously waiting for me. Five minutes earlier, on the walk from my car to the dormitory, I had run through my mind what I would say if I ran into my friends. But my plan to come back at an obscure time didn't work well after being away for four days.

Since I didn't really want to lie, I figured that all I needed to do was tell the exact story, only changing a few details. My story couldn't be too specific and it couldn't be too vague. The story had to be believable. When I got to the parts of the story that weren't 100% true, I had to move through them without hesitating. If I hesitated, I knew that it would create doubt and then my secret was in jeopardy.

"You will never believe it. The craziest thing happened to me," I said as I sat down in an empty chair next to them. "Late on Thursday night I went to Steak and Shake to study for my exam. I ordered my frisco melt with a chocolate shake and went to find a seat. But you guys know, the place is so small that there were no open tables. I saw this girl sitting at a booth by herself. She was a bit older but I figured I would just say hello and see if she would let me sit with her. So I walked over and asked if she minded me sitting with her since there was no other place to sit down. She looked up and had this beautiful smile on her face. She said, 'sure.'"

I was shocked the story was just rolling out of my mouth. At first I had this feeling of dishonesty, but as I kept going, it felt so normal as if I had completely transformed into a different personality.

"Her name was Susan," I proceeded with my nearly true story. "And she was a master's student. Somehow we just kept chatting instead of studying and chatting turned into flirting. And next thing you know, I am in my car following behind her car to the master's students' dorms thinking, 'Holy shit. I can't believe she just invited me over to her place.'"

"Oh my gosh, are you serious?" Sarah gasped with a look on her rosy-cheeked face like a deer caught in the headlights of an oncoming car. Sarah was the sweetest girl. She was one of those people that you could trust with your life. A wholesome person,

Sarah was a bit nerdy and had lived her life up to this point very safely, by the rules.

"And next thing you know, we are making out on her couch. Everything happened so fast," I said.

"Wait, what happened? Did you guys go all the way?" my roommate asked as he punched his fist into his other hand. I paused and shot them a look like I did go all the way because it was really hard for me to lie. "You did, didn't you?" he asked.

I bit my lower lip and grinned like I couldn't believe it myself. "I lost my v-card," I said.

"Holy shit," Sarah yelled loudly immediately cupping her hand over her mouth as everyone in the lounge paused to look over at our small pow wow in the corner.

"I stayed the night and then went to class directly from her place on Friday. I grabbed a change clothes from our room in the afternoon when you were at class and then went back to her place. We ended up hanging out all weekend. So that is why you guys didn't see me. It was one of the most random weekends in my life."

I knew giving too many details may seem strange to just volunteer about this type of story so I steered clear from giving away too much. It was all true. Except the minor details that Susan was really Gary and that I had met Gary online only hours before meeting him at Steak and Shake. But I had pulled it off. My secret was safe.

SEXUAL EXPLORATION

My exploratory experience with Gary lasted several weekends. Only this time I didn't have to sneak away. I told Sarah and my roommate that I was going to Susan's place. After telling them where I was going, I sensed their confusion, knowing that we only had a couple of weekends before winter finals and Christmas break. But for the first time in my life I felt that I could explore a part of me that I had repressed. Doing well on final exams was the last thing on my mind.

Each weekend we shared, Gary's egocentric personality chiseled away at my self-confidence. But my strong desire to explore my newfound sexuality overrode my ability to escape his hurtful disrespect.

"You are so skinny," Gary said to me as he laughed out loud on the last night we were together. "We should get you a cheeseburger."

We ended up in Gary's bed and the look in his eyes proved he only wanted one thing. The smell of Gary's cigarette smoke lingered in the small bedroom. I wasn't quite sure what I should be doing as Gary began aggressively pulling off my clothes. I felt frail compared to him. His shorter but broader frame appeared bloated, like he had drunk a lot of beer during his past four college years. The light-colored hair on his head was thinning and most likely would become bald in a few years.

"When is your dick going to start growing? It looks really small," Gary blurted out to me before anything happened. I immediately felt ashamed and embarrassed. Was this what sex with a man was supposed to be like? Aggressive, inconsiderate, impersonal, uncomfortable?

My naked body curled up as a protection mechanism to shield against the pain. My tear ducts activated and I was scared. Even though Gary watched me recoil, he proceeded to sickly laugh at me while I retreated to the far corner of the bed pushed into the corner of the room.

I shut my eyes and was discouraged about what I had done. I became uncertain if exploring my sexuality with a man was really what I wanted. The Catholic church flashed into my mind, along with the horrible guilty feelings that I had growing up, praying that I was not an outcast. I remembered the notes I wrote to myself praying that I was not gay.

Gary had gone outside behind his apartment to smoke a cigarette. I was alone. I quickly pulled my underwear back on. I put on my socks and pulled my jeans back up over my legs. And I picked up my sweater and pulled it on over my head. I wanted to escape before Gary came back inside.

As I passed by a mirror beside Gary's door before exiting his room, I could see my reflection. I paused and I looked into my red eyes. "Who are you? What the hell are you doing?" I asked myself with disappointment.

The cold air surrounded me as I pulled the front door shut. A stream of warm moisture rolled down my cheeks while I briskly walked to the parking lot.

I sat down into my cold car and the digital clock on the dash-board read 12:10 am. I placed my hands over my face, feeling the dampness from my tears and sat in silence. After wiping my face a few moments later, I began the two-hour drive to my parents' house for the holiday break. I was sad and ashamed, unsure of my own identity. I wanted to tell someone so badly, but I was alone.

LIQUID CONFIDENCE

"SO, WHERE ARE you going?" my mother asked, confused. This was the first time she had heard that I would be going somewhere for New Year's Eve. Previously, she had thought I would be home with her and my father.

"I'm going to Toledo with my friend from Fort Wayne. He is the one I went out with in Fort Wayne that night I came home late after the end of the semester. I met some of his friends and they have friends in Toledo that are throwing a New Year's party," I explained, using my late-night arrival from Gary's place a week and a half earlier as the cornerstone of my made-up story.

"Are you going to stay the night there? Do you know the address? How will I know where you will be?" she said.

"Actually, I don't know where the place is in Toledo. I am meeting them at a grocery store parking lot in the neighborhood and then following them to the party since they are coming from Fort Wayne," I said. The partially true story just rolled out of my mouth. "I think they are staying the night, but I probably will come back home tonight. Can I bring the bag phone with me so I have a phone in case I need to call you?" I asked, trying to make her feel better. She was clearly a little freaked out.

"Yes, I think you should take the phone with you. Please pay attention to the other drivers on the road. Especially on your way back home. It is New Year's," my mom said. "I love you."

"I love you, too," I said before I walked into the garage and shut the door. I grabbed the bulky car phone out of my mom's car. It was zipped into a black leather bag. The cold, dry air brushed against my exposed face as I walked outside to my car in the driveway.

My car headlights lit up the rural road in front of me as I sped away from my childhood home. "Gosh, it's kind of scary at how good I have become at making up stories," I thought as the moonlit countryside rushed by.

The drive wasn't that far. I met up with Jeremy and hopped into his car. We picked up his friend Aaron in a neighboring town before making our way to Toledo.

Jeremy was about four years older than Aaron and me. Jeremy was overweight and didn't take care of his body. You could sense that he lacked self-esteem when he would make negative comments about himself. He wore oversized shirts that sort of looked like a dress after they passed over his protruding stomach.

Jeremy was my first gay friend. He was someone close to my age who was experiencing something similar to what I was experiencing. However, Jeremy had told his family that he was gay. It scared me to death to think about telling my family. He was in a different mind space than I was, but he could relate, since he had been in my shoes. I know that Aaron was not out of the closet to anyone. So he and I were in the exact same spot. Both trying to discover who we were.

As we got closer to the club, my heartbeat got a little faster. I became a little irritable as my body started to heat up. I didn't know what to expect. It was a whole new world and I had to trust that it would be fun. But all of the thoughts that I have had before this moment rushed into my mind. My aunt and cousins live in Toledo. What if I saw them? What if my mom found out where I was?

We pulled into the dark parking lot filled with many cars next to the club. I was surprised to see the place so busy. I had expected only a few other outcasts would be at this club. Other people like us. Once Jeremy parked, he pulled out a small pint of vodka from his coat and offered it to us.

"Sweet!" I blurted out as I grabbed the thin glass bottle with the red label of Smirnoff. I tipped the bottle back to take a small swig and instantly felt my throat heat up as the liquor went down into my stomach. The pungent smell of vodka came up through my nose and burned my nostrils. My face shriveled up and I shook my head quickly back and forth, trying to shake away the taste of the alcohol.

Aaron was reluctant to take the bottle as we passed it around, so Jeremy and I kept taking turns swallowing swigs. My head started to tingle as the medicine was working. I knew that I wouldn't be able to drink inside, so I figured I would need to stock up now.

As we got out of the car, we threw our coats back inside the vehicle. I crossed my arms over my chest as the cold air surrounded my bare skin. We quickly walked across the parking lot. Even though we were downtown, I looked around and saw a bunch of abandoned buildings. It felt unsafe, so I made sure I kept my eyes on the lookout.

We approached a building with no windows along the concrete block facade that looked like it had been abandoned. We walked around the corner and approached a steel metal door painted bright red with only a long, vertical handle welded on the front.

"We are going in here?" I asked my buddies, confused. There was no way we were able to go in there.

Jeremy popped a quick smile and as he opened the heavy metal door, a faint electronic beat began to slide out from the building and into my ears. We stepped through the doorway and into a dimly lit space with a small window cut into the side of one of the walls. The metal door closed behind us as our eyes adjusted to the space.

"Hey, loves. Welcome to Bretz," someone with a very deep voice said from behind the small window. I had to lean around the edge of the opening to see who was speaking. The wrinkles on my forehead bunched together as my eyes opened widely in astonishment.

Her curly white hair was huge and was spread out as wide as it was tall in every direction. Her bright pink lipstick popped from her powdered white face and rosy red cheeks. Her ruffled hot pink dress looked like a lampshade that tightly formed around her large breasts and sides, hugging her figure, and then it opened up as it draped toward the floor.

"It will be ten each," she said. I reached into my back pocket to grab my wallet.

"Hi, honey. What is your name?" she said, directing her face toward me. My eyes must have been huge as she began talking to me. I felt like someone had just tasered me as I stood there staring back at her unable to talk. My limbs and my facial expression were completely frozen.

"Hi. My name is Cory." I timidly managed to get out after a few seconds of delay. I had been used to giving a fake name online so no one in the area would have any information about me. So it felt really uncomfortable to give away my real name.

"Hi, Cory, my name is Trixie." Her masculine voice flowed out as her pink lips pursed and her thick lashes fluttered like they were fanning me. "I'm going to need to see your ID, love."

My wallet had been open, so I reached in and pulled out my driver's license. I handed her the laminated card and also reached in to get a ten-dollar bill to pay the cover charge. Trixie gave me back my ID and said, "Hold out your left arm, cutie." She proceeded to put a green band around my wrist. She gave Aaron a green band also and Jeremy received a yellow band since he was over the age of twenty-one.

"Have fun, boys," Trixie said. The 's' on the end of the word 'boys' sounded like a 'z' and vibrated for a couple seconds. As we began to move down to the end of the hallway, the electronic bass began to get louder and louder.

"You guys ready?" Jeremy asked both Aaron and me, like he was ready for the big reveal. Jeremy was relaxed since he had been there several times before. But this was Aaron's first time at a gay bar also. We both flashed slight smiles, but you could tell we had no clue what to expect. We were newbies in every sense of the word.

COME ON BARBIE, LET'S GO PARTY

JEREMY PUSHED OPEN the metal door as the dance music now pulsated full volume. The large, square space was dark, but bright colored lights danced through the sparsely foggy air. There were five to six high top tables in front of us occupied by guys standing around with a glass in their hands. Beyond the tables was a larger open space with only a few people dancing. I surveyed the room. Most people congregated around the far edges of the room where the spinning lights weren't as bright.

Aaron and I followed Jeremy toward a long bar. As we moved in a single-file line, I sensed a collection of curious eyes locking in on us. Like we were fresh meat for the predators hiding behind the bushes and trees waiting to pounce.

Aaron and I stayed close to Jeremy as we maneuvered our way through the crowd in front of the bar. I felt much looser than I would have if I hadn't had the confidence boost in Jeremy's car before we entered. Other people's shoulders and arms brushed up against me as I squeezed through the group of guys standing around chatting with their friends.

As I passed, many of them would turn and look into my eyes. My eyes locked in with some guys for a split second, but then I looked down since it was awkward to make eye contact. But I was certainly curious. I wanted to go stand somewhere along a wall and do what most other people in the bar were doing. Checking everyone out. Jeremy finally managed to get to the front of the bar and ordered us some sodas while Aaron and I stood behind him.

"Wow, there are more people here than I thought," I said into Aaron's ear as he awkwardly leaned over so he could hear me. It was like his body had turned into a stiff robot. Aaron just nodded.

Jeremy turned around through the crowd at the bar and handed us a soda. Since I didn't know what else to do, I just put my lips on the straw and sipped on the brown drink. The sugar from the soda helped take the vodka taste out of my throat. Jeremy headed for the back wall of the dance floor, where it was darker. Aaron and I were like his cute little dogs on leashes being pulled behind him.

The night was still young as we sat down on some boxes against the wall. The light was dim in the back area where we were sitting, but we could see out onto the dance floor and beyond into the bar area with the high tables.

A sense of relief rushed through me, feeling safer with my back facing the wall. I could smell the musty, warm air that whiffed past our faces as many guys passed by. I noticed that we were in a direct traffic pattern that led back to the bathroom. Not such a bad spot to be, I thought. Now I could sit back and watch people pass like they were on display. I quickly caught onto the game.

"Holy crap, I am in public with other gay people," I thought. My shoulders and upper back remained tense. My mind raced back to my childhood when my male peers ridiculed me for having a high-pitched voice and for having friends who were girls. I felt this overwhelming sense that I had to act masculine around other gay people. That I had to act like a man because my mind had worked hard to not let others think that I was gay. I pressed my lips together tightly and clenched my jaw as a stern look came over my face. My chest puffed out slightly, asserting my manhood.

I had to act cool. I didn't want someone thinking that I was girly. I didn't want anyone to see me and think "faggot" or "gay" or "queer." I was just a normal, straight-acting guy from a rural farm town in Ohio who had macho friends. I wanted people to see a boy who was smart and talented. To see me as normal.

The music became slightly louder and more people started to move onto the dance floor. I loved the music that was playing, but it was all music that I would get made fun of if anyone back home heard me listening to it. I couldn't nod my head or move around like I was enjoying it because someone may think I am gay. I was so scared of my own identity I wasn't even comfortable owning it in a supposedly safe space.

...All that she wants is another baby...

It was one of my favorite songs after another.

...Come on Barbie, let's go party...

I was so torn. I wanted to get up and dance. Aaron and Jeremy looked like they were going to be attached to the box for the entire evening. If I did get up and dance, everyone would certainly look at me.

While I was deep in my head staring at the dance floor, a shadow grew closer from our right.

"Hey, how are you?" the shadow's voice said. I turned my head up to see beautiful white teeth and dreamy brown eyes gazing down at me in what appeared to be its own warm, personalized greeting. "My name is Jason."

Jason's soft cheeks were slightly flushed from moving around on the dance floor just moments before. My curious eyes had been drawn to his sweet smile from across the room and noticed his shaved head and overall shorter frame smoothly move to the fun beats.

My heart fluttered as he cautiously sat down in the small space next to me. I felt the pressure in my chest while I introduced myself. It felt like my very first junior high school dance. Only this time my eyes continued moving around the room to make sure no one noticed me.

It was difficult to hear Jason over the booming music, so he suggested we move to an area further away. Jason was at ease in this space and knew where to take me. I nodded to Jeremy and Aaron as they watched us get up and walk to a darker, less crowded area of the bar.

We stood facing each other against a brown brick wall further away from the dance floor. Our smiles flirted back and forth as we exchanged nervous banter about how we had gotten to the bar that evening. Mostly what I shared with Jason that night was true, even though it was almost too easy to withhold specific facts like my last name and the name of my hometown. My mind couldn't let go of the thought that he may potentially know someone that knew me.

Even though I wasn't able to share everything about myself with Jason, my eyes certainly were sharing more than my words were. His eyes were talking back as they blinked and warmed up my soul. Jason sensed I needed to release the nervous energy that had built up over the past couple of hours. He gave me a coy look, grabbed my cold hand and led me to the dance floor.

As I began to slowly shift my weight from side to side, the tension in my shoulders and back began to ebb away. My body temperature heated up as my limbs loosened to the beat of the music.

Our smiles turned into graduated laughter with our eyes locked in on each other. It seemed the rest of the world faded away. As each new song filled the room, the grips that once locked up my mind so tightly began to loosen. I was becoming free one song at a time.

Five. Four. Three. Two. One. Happy New Year!

The lights had dimmed and I faintly heard cheers around me. Our bodies slowed as the music stopped. Without hesitation, my hands pulled around Jason's sweaty body. My face leaned down to meet Jason's and my eyes closed as our salty lips gently collided. Shiny confetti rained down from the ceiling above and brushed past our locked faces.

My body tingled with adrenaline. The world began to slowly spin around us in the middle of the dance floor. We were locked in.

On the cold, dark drive back to my parent's house later that evening, my smile beamed as brightly as my headlights. I relived that kiss over and over in my head and I squeezed my shoulders forward with excitement as both hands held the steering wheel. My soul was buzzing. I felt human.

Once I pulled into my parents' driveway, my shoulders and back instantly tightened. Nervous energy began pulsing through my chest. The beautiful flower that had opened up to take in the rays of sunlight had closed almost in an instant. I quietly opened my parents' door and told my sleeping mother that I safely arrived back home just as I always had done.

I lay down in my warm bed and stared up at the ceiling painted in twilight. Was tonight just a dream? I wanted it to be real, but the thick protection barriers had risen back up. Feelings of guilt pressed hard on my internal organs. I held my chest, attempting to soothe the pain. I took a slow breath to process it all. But now

I was wrought with fear and I prepared to make sure my story about the night sounded real.

Hiding became a survival tactic, and I was exhausted. I began to believe true authenticity only occurred behind red metal doors. I thought it wasn't worth the pain to share my authenticity with my family.

Several weeks later, when I returned back from holiday break, I gave into my guilt. I wanted to be normal like everyone else. I felt macho-ness would cure me and I could lock away the guilty feelings forever if I joined a fraternity. Having frat moments with brothers I had always wished for would surely shake the gay away.

LET'S PLAY A GAME

THE FRIENDSHIP BETWEEN Sarah and I grew slowly after we met during our freshman year at Ball State University. Sarah became a Resident Assistant during our sophomore year and spent most of her time studying and taking care of her residents. I moved into the fraternity house with forty of my fraternity brothers. Joining the fraternity opened up so many friendship circles and opportunities to become involved in other student organizations.

But Sarah and I both knew we had a strong bond from the beginning. Besides the fact that we were born on the exact same day—I was only a couple hours older—we enjoyed meeting up for meals and we also shared a couple of classes.

Sarah was calm, steady, and a great listener. She wasn't a big partier like I had become, so it was really nice to have a friend outside of the wild fraternity life that was now a big part of my college experience. She was someone to share deeper conversations with, which we both really enjoyed.

During my junior year, I scored my own room in the fraternity house. My friend Sarah was serving her second year as a Resident Assistant in undergraduate dormitories that were located directly across the street from my fraternity house.

"Let's play a game" I said. Sarah noticed my face had turned a light shade of red, but figured it was because I had been quickly taking down a full bottle of chilled Pinot Grigio that I had snuck over into her room in my backpack.

I told her that we were going to play a guessing game: "Guess what's on my mind." I explained that she would think of something she wants to tell me, but I would have to guess what she was thinking after a series of clues. Sarah sat motionless with a puzzled look on her face.

After I told her that I would guess first, Sarah moved off of her twin bed and adjusted herself into a cross-legged position across from me on the maroon-colored shag rug that covered the center of the tile floor. She looked up at the cinder block wall deep in thought and agreed to play the random game.

It was only an hour earlier that I got off the phone with her offering to come over and keep her company while she worked. I hung up the phone and my nerves were shot. I sat in silence in my recliner chair, thinking of a way to tell her. But this moment had been building up for years.

Once she was ready, Sarah began to tell me progressive clues about her main thought. I told her my guess after each clue, and when it was wrong, I would tip up the clear, glass bottle and take a giant swig of the sweet, white wine. After several clues, a light buzz filled the crown of my head.

I was proud of myself that the game that I made up only minutes prior actually allowed me to drink more. I eventually guessed the right answer, that she was excited about all the work we had been doing for my bid for President in the University-wide Student Government Association election coming up in several weeks.

But the thought of all the work ahead of us seemed so minimal compared to all of the nervous energy that I had been exhausting to block out the thoughts and feelings about my sexuality. I had done such a great job of filling up my mind space with activities and events over the past several years to distract my authentic self from showing up.

My struggle was invisible. Yet, the insecurity and self-doubt that bubbled up inside became too heavy to carry alone. The student newspaper interviewed me each week for the upcoming election. I began to walk around campus and envision everyone knowing my struggle. My college career would be ruined.

Sarah settled into her seated position and began to guess what was on my mind. She wasn't able to drink any of the wine I brought into her dorm room since she was on duty for her entire building, so she drank swigs of Diet Coke out of a can.

The country apple scent from the burning candle nearby entered my nose and the floor lamp in the corner dimly lit up the room. I could hear Vertical Horizon softly jamming out of Sarah's CD player from behind her. My breathing sped up.

I told her that I was excited about the upcoming election. She shook her head knowing how vague that clue was and not understanding where I was guiding her. With my nerves beginning to grip my stomach, I told her that her friendship meant a lot to me.

Sarah's face softened and she leaned forward to give me a hug. She felt my skin had heated up and could see the beads of sweat forming on my forehead. As she sat back down with a half-smile on her face anticipating my next clues, her eyes softened and sent me love.

I then told Sarah that I've always known that I have been different than other people. Sarah shook her head slowly and paused, not ready to share what she was thinking. My shoulders and back tingled with fear and my face turned numb.

"I've had feelings that I have had trouble understanding myself," I told her. I paused, sensing my eyes begin to well up. I clamped my hands together and looked down at the soft rug taking a deep inhale. And then I continued, "But I need to talk with someone about it."

"After I became homecoming king this past fall, everyone on campus knows who I am. You have seen it: Beautiful girls have begun following me around and come up to me at our parties to talk with me. I like them, but they have always just felt like friends to me.

"It wasn't something that I consciously thought about, but my eyes have always noticed the guys. It has been normal for me to notice features of men. Facial features, short hair, muscles, masculinity. I notice it all. I notice women also, but I would only notice how nice they were and not what they looked like."

I reached up to wipe away the tears that had begun to slide down my cheeks. Sarah got onto her knees and crawled over to me.

"Oh sweetie," she said. My head dropped down and she wrapped her love around me, pulling my body in close with hers. "I love you," Sarah whispered into my ear as she delicately held me. I began to weep. I entered an uncontrollable sob as the years of tension I had carried around began to wash away.

Sarah reached over to grab a tissue from her nightstand and I wiped my wet face with my damp hands. She looked into my pink eyes and told me that my secret would stay with her forever. My heart warmed and my soul comforted, knowing that it would be ok.

BIG MAN ON CAMPUS

Now that the emotional grip that plagued my mind had eased, I could pivot my energy by focusing on winning the largest prize at our university, Student Government Association President. The build-up over the next several weeks proved intense, with speaking engagements, newspaper interviews, and televised debates against a fierce opponent who was majoring in political science. Most of my life was pushed out into the eyeballs of over 20,000 students, faculty, and administration. But only one other person knew all of me.

On election night, my mother and father made the two-hour drive from their home to take my entire team out to dinner after the voting had ended. Even with the adrenaline still pumping through our exhausted bodies, we were able to catch our breath eating unlimited breadsticks and salad before anxiously waiting for the news.

The large television room of my fraternity house was filled past capacity with my fraternity brothers, campaign team, and close friends spilling into the connected kitchen and dining room. The buzzing energy and loud chatter was electrifying as the television showed the election night coverage from the student news television station. I paused for a moment to survey the room, seeing the smiles of friends who had volunteered their time to help me achieve a goal. Even if I didn't win, I knew that we had already accomplished such an incredible feat.

The cell phone of the news reporter who was covering my campaign began to beep. She was standing near the low sitting couch where my team was anxiously resting. A collective silence spread through the warm room as she flipped open the phone. She exchanged a few words and then reached the phone out toward me. Her face was blank as I stood up to grab the phone out of her hand.

The television had been muted and the packed room had now become completely silent. Everyone's eyeballs were transfixed on all of my movements. My hand shook as I pulled the phone up to my ear and said hello.

After a few seconds of listening to the calm voice on the other line, I dropped my head and turned away from the onlooking crowd. I slowly pulled the phone away from my ear and flipped the device closed, gently setting it on the long table. I raised my head and took a long look at the condensation that had covered the window in front of me as I breathed in one of the deepest breaths that I had ever taken.

I turned around and the adrenaline in my body exploded as I launched myself off the carpet with my arm extended into the air. "We did it!" I yelled at the top of my lungs. Everyone jumped to their feet, arms flung into the air, and the room erupted into one of the loudest simultaneous roars that I can remember. Everyone began throwing out high-fives to each other and my team wrapped their arms around me as we all jumped around in pure joy.

THE LAST STAND

As THE YEAR went on, I became wrapped up in appearances with the University President, writing a weekly column in the student newspaper, attending events and meetings, and, of course, completing schoolwork. The weekly parties in my fraternity house became my stress relief. Girls from all over campus would flock to our house.

It was carefree fun for me to chat and flirt with the girls. But their flirting would never work. After a few months, a quiet storyline began to slowly form throughout various friendship circles. One evening while hanging out with my fraternity brothers, they began to joke around about me never having a girlfriend or having girls stay the night.

I immediately felt my stomach turn over and I tried to prevent my face from turning red. I let out a breathy laugh with a cracked smile on my face. The emotional pressure that I had once conquered had rushed back into my heart. It hadn't even occurred to me that people would notice that I had always been single. I quickly needed a strategy. I had to make sure my story was completely believable so no one would see any cracks.

In November of my senior year, I met a beautiful girl whose sorority often paired with my fraternity for events. She was the perfect, All-American girl. Sweet, funny, athletic, committed, and from a loving, Midwest family. Her light brown hair came down just past her shoulders. Her face was soft with slightly rosy cheeks. Her bright, brown eyes glowed and her perfect, white smile was enough to make every guy on campus swoon.

Lisa made me laugh and I felt carefree when I was around her. As Lisa and I became closer, Sarah didn't quite know what to say.

When she saw us together, Sarah's eyes would narrow. But she never said anything to me as she watched this storyline play out.

Around Christmas time, Lisa came home with me to meet my parents. My parents had gone to sleep and I was sleeping out on the pull-out couch alone in the living room while Lisa slept in the twin bed in my childhood room. As I lay in the darkness, I heard Lisa tiptoe around the corner and she stealthily crawled next to me under the warm blankets.

The cheap mattress coils creaked when I rolled over to greet her. My body touched hers as our lips converged. Our breaths came in through our noses while our kissing intensified. I rolled over and straddled her laid-out body. She was beautiful. With a flirting smile, I grabbed the sides of her soft pajama shirt. After I slowly pulled her shirt over her head, exposing her bare stomach and laced, cream colored bra, her eyes instantly turned lustful. I sensed she was ready to take this as far as she could.

An awkward sense of pressure shifted through my chest. My hands became moist while I struggled to think of what to do next. It felt like I was being forced to touch her delicate skin and then slowly moved my hand up over her bra. The uneasy feeling pulsating in my head made me hesitate. My mind was uncontrollably rejecting everything. My heart raced and I lowered myself back to her side taking my hands off her chest.

Lisa's eyes pulled down with a confused look and she paused waiting for me to say something. My mind raced to come up with a response to what had just happened. I didn't want her to feel rejected. "I am Catholic and want to save it for marriage," I calmly crafted.

As those believable words left my mouth, I knew what my truth was. That being attracted to boys certainly was not a choice, but an overwhelming feeling from deep within. This moment was my last stand. And ironically, trying to conform to society gave me time to find what I didn't want. It was time to stop the fighting.

I had taken one of the biggest steps in my life. The person in the mirror was all of me. But I had waited to share this with my mother because once my mom knew, I couldn't just take it back "Just kidding mom. I was attracted to boys but now I am back to liking girls." I had to first find my truth. All of my truth.

NO MATTER WHAT

Two weeks before I would pack up all of my belongings and drive across the country to New York City to begin my career, I attended my sister's friend's wedding with my mother. "I don't think this will ever happen for me," I thought as I watched the bride slowly step down the center aisle to meet her husband-to-be at the altar. It was a dream of mine, but I didn't know if that dream would ever come true.

A dark emotional cloud hovered over me as I watched all of the reception guests laughing, smiling, and living it up on the dance floor from across the large, glass-ceiling atrium space. Marrying another man was illegal. I would have to live in hiding if I was committed to another man.

As I sat there watching the carefree fun continue, it felt like my demise was staring at me in the face. That I had to accept the fact that I wouldn't be happy. Having our engagement picture in the newspaper. Having people celebrate our wedding. To be able to celebrate our authentic selves in an authentic relationship validated in front of God and everyone else.

My mother sensed something was on my mind during the quiet ride back home around midnight. I knew the entire drive home that I needed to tell her. It would be a perfect scenario to tell her before I left for New York in two weeks so that way if she wasn't accepting, I could escape. But she needed to know what I had been feeling for most of my life. She knew me better than anyone in the entire world, but she didn't know all of me.

When we arrived back home, I turned on the lights to the second living room that we rarely used. The house was quiet and we were alone. After sitting on the couch for five minutes, I asked her to come into the living room and sit down.

"What's wrong? You love weddings. You love receptions. You love dancing. You are usually the life of the party. Something is going on, Cory," she said. I wondered if she already knew what I was going to tell her. But I knew that my mother had grown up on a farm in rural northwest Ohio and probably didn't even know what the word gay meant. She probably thought it meant that someone was really happy. She hadn't knowingly been around gay people. It was never anything that remotely crossed her mind.

If I told her I knew my life would change forever. I looked down at the ground and my nerves were wracking. "Do I tell her? Or don't I tell her? Do I rip the Band-aid off? Just rip it off." If I didn't tell her, when would I tell her after moving to New York? Months, maybe years, could go by without her ever knowing.

"Mom, there is something that I have known about me for all of my life, but I just wasn't certain it was true. But I think now I know it's true." I paused to calm the nervous energy flowing through my veins as I shoved my sweaty palms under my thighs on the soft couch cushion. "The reason I wasn't able to have fun tonight was because I may never have those moments. The wedding. The reception." I looked back down at my feet and shook my head, knowing my truth was about to be exposed. I could no longer hide from the person who loved me the most in the world.

She listened intently to what I had to say as she sat across from me on the couch. My shoulders hunched forward and I shifted my body to the edge of my seat. "Mom, I think I am gay."

My mom looked at me shaking my head a little. "Cory, I love you no matter what." She stood up and walked over to me and put her arms around me as I buried my face in my hands. She could see the pain on my face. She could sense the years of stress, emotion, fear, and feeling scared that I had experienced. And in that moment, my life changed forever.

My mom knew that it didn't matter, just like if I were black or brown or had a disability. That even though she may not completely understand me, that she loved me no matter what. She loved me unconditionally. She wasn't just going through the motions to say, "I love you." She meant it. She felt it.

4
HOMECOMING KING

CHILDHOOD GUILT

I CAN STILL hear my neighborhood friend's dad yelling at me, "Don't ever come back to this house again!" The bright sun beamed down as I walked from my friend's house along the quiet, paved street to my house. "What will I tell my mom? What will she think?" I kept repeating over and over as tears of guilt rolled out of my eyes and down my cheeks. I turned the corner and stared at my house a hundred yards away.

I grew up in Montpelier, Ohio, a small town surrounded by farm fields located in the extreme northwest corner of the state. It is a quiet community with nearly 4,000 residents, a couple of stop lights and a handful of historic, downtown buildings occupied by small, local businesses. But while the town is small, the safe neighborhoods allowed us to roam around carefree, not having to worry about our safety.

My body quivered with each slow step I took. The consequences of what I had done when I got home would be harsh. I was thankful my father was not home yet from work, since his punishment would be ten times worse than my mother's.

I was a skinny kid at six years old. I couldn't explain why I did those things. I was just playing with the neighborhood boy, who was a year younger. We often took baths together and my friend's mom would leave us alone in the bathtub while she worked in the kitchen.

We rolled cars around the bathtub and then began rolling cars onto each other. VROOM! I rolled the car over my friend and we would giggle. I moved the car down his stomach and then rolled it below the water over his midsection.

While we both were still giggling, I reached out my other hand and touched his naked body. My actions were purely impulsive. I couldn't understand why I did it. It just happened. It felt natural to me. It wasn't malicious in any way. And my friend giggled like we normally did while playing.

My friend then put his hand on my naked body under the water in a very playful way. It was fun. I was too young for it to feel any other way than having fun. After a few moments of touching each other, my friend's mom must have heard what was happening and barged into the bathroom.

"What are you doing?" she shouted in a raised voice. "Get out of the bathtub now."

My friend and I jolted in the water. We didn't know why she was so angry. We grabbed towels laying on the floor outside of the bathtub and proceeded to dry off. As she stormed out, we were a little confused but looked at each other and started laughing under the towels.

About thirty minutes later, my friend's dad arrived home early from work. I'll never forget the look of fear on his face when he slammed open the door to my friend's room and came right at me with his finger pointed. I felt like I was in a cartoon show and he was the scary villain trying to capture me. My friend was startled and remained motionless as my head dropped down and I slowly walked out of his room.

My mother was waiting for me in the kitchen near the table when I opened the door from the garage. My stomach quivered as I tried to catch my breath between my sobs. I slowly looked up at my mother. I was surprised to see a look of concern on her face instead of a look of disappointment. I was anticipating that I would immediately be sent to my room as punishment.

She must have known what had happened before I came home. She told me to go sit on the couch and calm down.

My mother never talked about what had happened. She must have known at that moment that I was different from the other boys. I don't think she ever told my father. That was the last time I ever visited my neighborhood friend.

Even though my early childhood friend and his family lived nearby, after that moment, we never talked again. And nearly every day, as I passed his home to go into town or into school, I was reminded of the shame and embarrassment that I had endured.

UNLIKELY HEROES

UNFORTUNATELY, THE SCHOOL bus didn't stop directly in front of my house to quickly escape after school. All of the kids got off the bus together in a central neighborhood location and then we walked to our respective houses. I was in the seventh grade and my sister had sports practice after school, so I went home alone each day.

Jack lived down the street from my house and had to walk in the same direction as me to get home. He was a year younger, but he was a thick, chubby kid who had grown taller than me. Jack was rough-looking and always came to school in noticeably soiled clothes.

Once the weather became warmer, Jack began to wait for me to get off the bus each day. Once off the bus, he made sure that he walked close to me and would glance back at the bus until it turned the corner. He waited for the moment right to begin badgering me.

One particular afternoon, I had to hunch over as I walked to prevent the weight of the books in my backpack from pulling my scrawny frame backwards. Once the bus was out of sight, Jack placed his hand on my shoulder and gave me a moderate push. The weight of the backpack swung my body sideways harder than normal.

"What's the matter, sissy? Are you scared of me?" Jack would say in a nasty tone as an evil grin appeared on his face. I would try to move away from him to the other side of the quiet neighborhood street. I looked around at the houses that lined the street, but didn't see anyone outside. Jack moved closer to me and continued to shove me. Each time, my athletic shoes shuffled on the gravel near the edge of the street and I would struggle to hold my balance.

"Jack, please stop it," I said politely in my prepubescent voice.

"Stop it," Jack mocked . He was like a hungry lion teasing his weak prey.

Once Jack saw that I wasn't far away from my house, he gave me one last shove that was much harder than the others. My head bounced to one side as my body flew sideways. My hands hit the rough asphalt first, then the momentum of my backpack pulled the side of my body over. Sharp pain shot through the side of my hip as I bounced on the hard surface. My head dropped and I looked down in embarrassment.

Jack laughed sinisterly as he stood over me watching me lay helplessly on the hard pavement. He pointed his chubby fingers down at me as he licked his lips and laughed. Once he got his fill of pleasure by watching his defeated prey, he continued on to his house down the street, still laughing.

I was terrified to defend myself even though I wanted to. I visualized me shoving him back, but I could see him becoming angry and pushing me back harder. I didn't want to get hurt so I tried to find ways to avoid Jack.

Jack's bullying continued for weeks. I began sitting in the front seat of the bus so I could be the first one off. Once I stepped off the bus, I began to run as fast as I could with my backpack heavily bouncing against my back. For the first week, my new strategy worked. I made it to my house before he could catch me.

However, one specific day during the last week of the school year, I could hear Jack's feet stomping into the asphalt behind me. His heavy breath became louder. He was determined this time to catch me. I felt Jack's approaching hand latch onto my backpack as he gave it a giant tug. My head snapped backward and my arms flew out to the sides. My body flailed and violently tumbled to the ground.

As I lay in the middle of the street staring up at the gray sky, I could see the frustration on Jack's face from not being able to catch me over the past week. In an instant, the front of his shoe forcefully landed into my side. As the sharp pain shot through my stomach and up into my chest, I could hear Jack sickly enjoying the agony he was creating. I recoiled trying to protect my body from any more blows. But as I lay there with him hovering over me, the evil sounds began to subside.

I began to imagine a circular alien spaceship piercing through the thick clouds above. Green and yellow lights were blinking from the bottom of the shiny metallic structure that appeared to be spinning counterclockwise. The craft quickly descended and I could hear a faint humming sound once the structure hovered twenty feet directly over Jack and me. A circular opening at the center opened up and a bright, yellow light beamed down on him.

Jack's eyes swelled as he looked up in terror. He panicked and began to run down the street. Just then, small, gray creatures slowly descended through the thick tubular beam of light. Their huge eyes dominated their wrinkled gray face and their heads made up half the size of their entire body. One after the other, about fifty in total quickly descended in choreographed order. They all looked at me lying on the ground on top of my backpack, almost reassuring me with their eyes that they would help me.

Once their short bodies touched the ground, their small feet propelled toward Jack as he clumsily ran as fast as he could. Jack turned around to see what was happening. But as he turned his head, his foot snagged on the back of his opposite leg and his body awkwardly flopped hard down to the ground. Jack skidded forward. He tried to get back up but the creatures had quickly caught up to him.

Their gray bodies surrounded Jack blocking my vision. "Cory! Cory! Help me!" I heard as his terrified voice cracked. The gray swarm began to move closer to the hovering craft with Jack lodged somewhere in the middle. Once the mob shifted under the tubular light, I saw Jack's stiff body float upward. Both his eyeballs and mouth were snapped open as far as they could go. His face was frozen like he had been zapped while he was yelling out for help.

Just as they had descended, each creature quickly rose back up within the bright yellow light and into the spaceship. As the last one entered the opening, the creature turned around and winked one of its large eyes at me. The circular door scissored closed and the spaceship launched straight up into the sky, vanishing quickly through the clouds.

I quickly turned my head to see if anyone else saw what I had. I shifted onto my hands and knees and slowly stood up. I glanced down the street and saw Jack's figure off in the distance walking away. He must have decided to leave me alone while my mind creatively imagined his fate.

And then I took one last look at the clouds. As I stood there, a slow grin filled my face. I had overcome my fear that day. I had defeated my enemy. The rest of the walk home was one of the best that I ever had.

GYM CLASS BATHING SUIT

WHILE I HAD my own troubles just trying to make it home each day after school, enduring the school day was even more difficult. Whether it was on the playground or during lunch time in the cafeteria, or even in the bathroom, I never knew where the next attack would come from.

Even though I loved being athletic and would sweat during gym glass, the moment I dreaded more than anything during the school day was taking a shower after class with my peers. Most of the boys just stripped off their sweaty clothes and walked their pale, naked tween bodies into the wide-open shower area. Multiple shower heads attached to the cinder block wall towards the top of the ceiling without any type of partition or barrier. It was one large room spraying out water on all sides.

My body trembled as I walked back to the locker room with the group of rowdy boys after class. While most of the other boys were talking to each other and laughing as they frolicked in the shower, I waited for the right opportunity to slide off my athletic shorts and quickly put my school clothes back on before anyone could see my exposed body.

I was always the first boy out of the locker room, until one day my macho gym teacher figured out that I was not showering. I could see the frustration on my teacher's face when he told me that I had to shower like all the other kids did. My face turned numb with fear and I felt like I was being punished for being me.

After gym class the following week, my gym teacher crossed his thick, muscular arms as his eyes followed me into the locker room, reminding me of what he told me last week. After all the other boys entered the shower, I looked around to make sure no one could see me in the far corner and took off my gym shorts and shirt. I wrapped a towel around my waist and struggled to slip my underwear off to make sure my midsection wasn't exposed. Then I pulled out my bathing suit that I had brought from home and pulled it up my thin, bird-like legs.

Boys were beginning to come out of the shower as I walked in with my head down avoiding making any eye contact. They immediately noticed I wasn't naked like them. And then I heard it.

"You're such a girl!"

"Sissy!"

The pain pelted me like they were throwing rocks. One after another, the boys left. I quickly became the last person in the shower room. I wanted so badly to say something back to the other boys, but I was lost in the pain. I tried to hold back my emotions, but the rocks penetrated my protective shield. The steamy shower streamed onto my face, masking my tears. It was just another reminder that I didn't fit in.

The rest of the day I was on the verge of breaking down. The boys later doubled down and quietly launched their attacks. I looked over and saw one of the boys staring at me. He wiggled his head and silently mouthed the word "faggot" to me. My eyes rolled back and I quickly looked away. There wasn't much I could do or say.

I arrived home later that day, ran to my room, and closed the door. Tears gushed out of my eyes as I buried my face into my pillow. The pain was too much to bear. I felt worthless. I felt there was no end in sight. That this pain would be here forever. I wondered how I would ever fit in.

MY SISTER'S SHADOW

MY SISTER IS eighteen months older than I am and growing up, she was always bigger, stronger, smarter, more athletic, and more perfect than me. At home, she was the perfect child, doing everything my parents asked of her. In the classroom, she got straight A's. And in athletics, she was the quintessential jock. She was the best female athlete at our high school in all sports seasons: volley-ball, basketball, and softball. One year she broke her finger early on in the softball season, so she became a track star.

She was voted most likely to succeed and most popular by her high school peers. She was voted onto the Homecoming Court in high school multiple years and then became Miss Montpelier, winning the local village pageant one summer. She would go on to become the valedictorian of her graduating class and won all sorts of academic and sports honors, including a volleyball schol-arship to a private university in Ohio.

And then there was little me. At home, I was the trouble-maker, frequently getting sent to my room for causing havoc. In the classroom, I did pretty well, but was often bored and found a way to get into trouble. During my freshman year of high school, I remember sitting on the bench on the basketball team hoping I wouldn't get called into the game since I was scared to play. I hadn't hit puberty yet, so I was still very short. Even though I would go on to become the salutatorian of my graduating class of 69 people, I was basically invisible. There was not even a chance I'd be voted most likely to succeed or best anything.

It was hard enough enduring the bullying during my formative years. But seeing my sister thrive and not have to endure any sort of hardship like I went through made it even more damning. It became a constant, visible reminder that I was weak. That I was not the same as everyone else. That I wasn't good enough.

In high school, I saw my classmates running around carefree just being typical teenagers. They didn't feel any societal judgment that they were different. They were just themselves: thinking about their upcoming football or basketball game, trying to figure out how to stay out late after prom so their parents wouldn't find out, or hanging out with their boyfriend or girlfriend.

And for the most part, all of my classmates had visible role models and influencers. They had people in their lives that they could look up to and mirror. Influencers and local role models like parents, teachers, coaches, and neighbors. Everyone was Caucasian and mostly lived in middle-income homes. Everyone looked like each other. For my peers, looking up to someone was subconscious.

But I didn't have the same experience. My father wasn't a role model. As the feelings that I couldn't explain to anyone bubbled up inside of me, how was I supposed to find someone whom I could trust? A role model that I could look up to? I didn't see anyone like me. A person who had endured the same struggle with their own sexuality.

Everyone saw my outward smile. But no one could see my internal struggle. No one was there to help me understand how to handle my emotions because no one knew about it. To help me figure out if it was even ok to have the feelings that I was having.

And if my secret escaped, it wouldn't be long before the entire town would know. Whispers. Gasps. Shaming, unaccepting stares. Hands clutching their pearls. I would become the grinch wrapped in a rainbow flag banished far from town.

MY ESCAPE

THE LOUD, ANTIQUATED bell rang and everyone filed out of three floors of classrooms. After most of my peers left, I exited the airy art room and walked through the museum-like hallways of the one-hundred-year-old high school building lined with rows of tall, gray metal lockers. My eyes slanted down at the polished concrete floor and I occasionally glanced up to make sure no one noticed me. The upper balcony to the theater was typically empty during the day, so when no one was looking, I snuck in through the light blue wooden doors and quickly closed them after I passed through.

I pushed the hinged wooden seat down in the last row of connected seats and settled onto the hard surface with my back up against the block wall of the quiet theater. The upper balcony only had ten rows and hung over the middle of the main floor. My eyes flipped up toward the empty stage in front of me and I let out a light laugh through my closed mouth.

It was only a month ago that I was up on stage during our annual high school musical. Our director had chosen a musical that featured only four male performers, Forever Plaid. I was devastated to learn that I was not selected as one of the featured performers after diligently practicing several weeks prior to tryouts for the baritone role. But since our director wanted to include as many students as possible, she cleverly created a customized pre-show show.

I certainly didn't want to be the appetizer for the main course, but my director pulled me aside to explain how hard it was to make the selection and exclude me from the top group of four performers. After she finished lamenting, her face lit up to tell me that she wanted me to be the master of ceremonies for the opening act. A ringleader of sorts. My face remained blank as I grabbed the pre-show script from her hand. I sported a half smile, thanked her and then turned around, feeling my eyes roll far up into my head as I walked away.

I walked out on stage in my black tailcoat tuxedo and top hat, forcing a smile to welcome everyone and to kick off the show. The pre-show show. The pre-show commenced as normal and I exited backstage. A little later, I reappeared through the center of the thick blue curtain to perform one of my main numbers. A group of formally dressed dancers were beginning to position themselves behind me as I started in with my lines.

However, once I was several lines into my main act, my mind went blank and I stopped. I turned around to the group on the stage and they looked at me in shock. My eyes flipped back into the obscenely bright spotlight pointed straight at me. My heartbeat pounding, my mind began racing, trying to remember what I was supposed to say next.

What happened next rolled out of me like I had practiced it ten times before. I bent over and began hysterically laughing out loud. And I told the audience the truth. That I had forgotten my lines. The crowd burst into laughter having no idea that this moment was certainly not going as planned.

With the adrenaline pumping through my chest and arms, I naturally walked off stage and into the amused audience. I looked toward the back of the dark room past the spotlight now following all of my movements and could see my director burying her face in her hands. The audience's laughter and positive energy fueled my soul.

If I had a religion, the theater would be my church and the stage would be my altar. Performing was my Sunday service. I began asking audience members if they could remind me of my lines and candidly bantering with them. They had to wipe away their tears and were hunched over in laughter. Even though I still had no clue of what I would do next, my mind became carefree. I had escaped my reality, even if just for a moment.

While I was having more fun with the audience than I ever could have imagined, I looked back to one of my friends who was a dancer on stage like it was all part of the act. And I asked everyone to help me out. My friend played along and threw out the words of my next line. It was like a file folder with my lines printed on a piece of paper appeared in my brain. After a few more moments of reveling in the situation, the show continued as planned.

SHOWING UP AS MYSELF

THREE YEARS LATER and one hundred and thirty miles away, I was standing in a dark suit on a completely different stage. Nine other male students stood next to me in a row across a stage that was over four times larger than my high school stage. I looked out at the 3,500 people that filled the airy auditorium. Nearly all of my one hundred fraternity brothers were seated in the first three rows, anxiously looking on to see who would become the university's next Homecoming King.

Earlier that week, each of the top ten candidates separately met with an alumni panel and the panel's opinions would represent the majority of the total score to determine the final winner. I walked across the thin carpeting of the Alumni Center and into the corporate-like meeting room that had one window leading out to the football field. I sat down in a chair positioned in the middle of the room facing a row of five distinguished alumni who were seated behind a long table with a bright red university banner hanging down in front.

Each visibly diverse panelist presented one question during the thirty-minute conversation. I remained calm during the basic, softball questions like, "How would you represent the university if you were Homecoming King?" and "What are your strengths?" The voices inside my head kept telling me to smile, to have fun. I had nothing to lose since I was the only junior candidate among nine seniors.

A middle-aged African-American mother of three children all under the age of ten gave me a warm smile before she provided me the final question. "What does empathy mean to you?" Each panelist's head slowly pivoted in unison toward me to see how I would react, like it was the climax of the entire interview.

I sat motionless in the cushioned chair as my brain exploded. The sides of my closed lips curled, shifting my cheeks upward, and I began to pull in the cool air through my nostrils. And then, just as clarity had filled my soul several years back after a moment of lapse on my high school stage, I entered a state of flow.

I described a moment helping my mother in her second-grade classroom. I was teaching her students how to make origami. As the children became frustrated by the intricate folding instructions, I would lower my presence to their level to listen and to understand how they felt. To support and to empower them to push through the adversity they were facing.

My perfect flow in front of the entire panel radiated my own truth. The painful path that I had traveled. Like I was going back to tell my younger, confused self that I would be ok. That being different is good. And that for the first time in my life, I didn't need permission to begin showing up as my authentic self.

As I calmly stood on stage four days later, the announcer named the top four male and female members of the Homecoming Court. My shoulders pulled back with arms at my side and my head held high, I stood firmly planted on the soft wood making up the stage's subfloor among the remaining candidates. I heard my friend's name announced as the Homecoming Queen and I glanced over to see her shocked face. I beamed, knowing it was the perfect selection.

My stomach turned over as she walked forward toward the crowd. I looked out at the warm lights beaming down at me and my throat began to throb thinking about how I got to this moment. Thinking to myself that life can pay out if you choose.

"And this year's Ball State University Homecoming King is...Cory Calvin!" the announcer's deep voice proclaimed.

My mind snapped out of a moment of contemplation. I looked over at the announcer with a look of confusion on my face. *Did I just hear my name?* The remaining group of candidates began to clap and looked my way. My fraternity brothers jumped out of their chairs with their arms extended.

I took a confident step forward. My teeth were exposed and my body tingled with nervous energy. I leaned my head down and a student representative placed a thick gold medal with a large red ribbon over my short hair. The Homecoming Queen walked over to give me a long, comforting embrace at the very edge of center stage.

And as I turned to face the jubilant crowd, I looked out in almost disbelief. A standing ovation. And a turning point on a path to begin discovering who I really was.

5
C.H.O

FROM CORNFIELDS TO WALL STREET

A s my father drove his freshly washed SUV on the expressway, pulling the large trailer toward the bright morning sun, I looked out the backseat window, remembering my high school show choir's final competition trip to New York City.

Our charter bus stopped across the Hudson Harbor for a photo opportunity of the awe-inspiring skyline on a clear, sunny spring day. I stood between my mother and father with my long arms around their shoulders, gazing at the World Trade Center's infamous twin towers and said, "I'm going to live there one day."

My parents let out an "it's good to dream big" chuckle as I began to dream. They couldn't have imagined that four life-changing years later, we would be driving all of my possessions to the Big Apple to begin my career at a Wall Street firm.

My mother sat in the front seat fighting through thoughts of fear and apprehension. Her eyes watered, thinking back through the years of consistently telling me that I could do anything that I put my mind to during emotional moments when I felt I had no reason to be. She was my rock. My number one fan. Even though she was scared to death to lose me, she was proud as hell.

The rows of short, green corn stalks zipped by and nervous excitement buzzed through me. But my excitement wasn't because of the fact that I beat out many Ivy League candidates for a spot in the prestigious investment banking group. My excitement revolved around the relief of a fresh start. I visualized myself walking out of my apartment building, walking to work, never passing anyone that I knew. I could wear a rainbow flag around my shoulders and no one would flinch.

But I knew that several blocks before I got to the office, I would need to take off the rainbow flag and bury it deep into my backpack. I had to make an impactful first impression. I had to prove that I belonged.

A year into my career and I wasn't able to tell anyone at work about my sexuality or I'd be tossed in the trash just like my Managing Director tossed his loose change in his pocket into the trash can looking on with disgust. My Managing Director was renowned as one of the top deal makers on Wall Street. His thin frame shot straight up like a strong beanstalk and his dark, narrow mustache resembled that of a dictator. When he spoke, the deep bass of his voice reverberated in your ears, sending your brain a warning of "do not mess with me." A master of his craft, he had nerves of steel and most people in our own company feared him.

One afternoon I sat at the glass table in his corner office overlooking Radio City Music Hall. Our entire team was on an important call with one of our top clients. My laptop was open and I fed my Managing Director important figures from the bond model that I had built in the early hours of the morning, carrying over from the night before. The figures from my model were vital to finalize a multi-million-dollar deal.

His assistant, a middle-aged Polish woman from Queens, kept beeping in on the other phone line of the call box positioned in the middle of the circular table we were huddled around. I could see my Managing Director's head shake with utter annoyance as he pressed the ignore button on the phone. She attempted to call in on yet another line, but he ended up blocking all incoming lines.

His assistant's short silver hair appeared through the semi-transparent floor-to-ceiling window that separated the office from the internal hallway. She timidly knocked on the door and the door handle began to turn. Her head quietly appeared through the cracked door. Everyone in his office knew that his wife was in labor and could be having his first child at any moment.

His assistant's eyes quickly flipped between my Managing Director and the floor. Once he saw her, he jolted his long, thin arms straight out to the sides into the air and gave her a look of death. Our client's voice was streaming out of the speaker and my Managing Director reached down with his long pointy fingers to press the mute button. She proceeded to meekly deliver the once-in-a-lifetime message that his wife had been in labor and was about to deliver.

A loud scream erupted from his open mouth. He berated her for rudely interrupting the conference call, almost derailing a massive bond deal and quickly fluttered his hand, signaling he wanted her to leave. Defeated, she quickly turned and left the room. My colleague looked over at me in complete shock. I became paralyzed with fear.

This was a far cry from the corn fields I had come from. It really was a dog-eat-dog world here. Wall Street was not for the weak. And even though I couldn't believe some of the things I saw, it became apparent that this was the type of toughness that I had trained for. A toughness I learned through coping with the insecurities I felt deep within my soul. A defense mechanism. A hardening of my outer shell to survive.

It turns out that Wall Street was a perfect place for me to begin my career. A place where my toughened shell would shine through as a smart hard worker. It was a place where I could put my head down into my work and thrive. I was able to quickly master the corporate world, at least on the surface.

But even though my deeper soul wasn't ready to fully show up inside of the office, I was certainly ready to explore a part of me that I had buried for all of my life outside of the office. No more small town to watch my every move. No more newspaper articles featuring me. No one knew me.

It was time for me to explore the repressed me. When I left the office each night, I stripped away my corporate costume. The late evenings and weekends became my recess and Manhattan was my playground. Game on.

Chat rooms. Boys. Sex. Booze. Bars. Cute bartenders. Happy hours. Parties. Drag queens. Cover charges. Clubs. Downstairs. Cruisy bathrooms. Secret backrooms. Shirtless dancefloors. Pulsating music. Strobe lights. Go-go dancers. Hook ups. Drunk taxi rides. Hell's Kitchen. Chelsea. West Village. 3am pizza.

New friends. Dates. Gay happy hours. Gay house parties. Gay volleyball leagues. Gay pride parades. The brilliantly colored pride flag floating past me as I stood among the millions of people that looked like me. All different shapes, sizes, colors, religions, genders. Yet we were all one, standing together, living our truth together.

My Monday morning ritual was locked in. Pick up my cheap, three sugar black coffee at my favorite street vendor and then begin editing all of the stories from the past couple days. Bar names, people, locations, and potential events would all need to be erased and new descriptions were created. I took a few moments to practice the newly created details in my head before walking into the office building to make sure my story naturally flowed for the age-old water cooler questions.

Even though I had officially walked out of one closet, the corporate closet remained a comfortable place for me to hide for several years. It continued to feel safe to turn a piece of me off each day. Safe to not bring my full self to work.

But over time, the energy I spent preventing my whole self to show up at work began to wear me down. My internal struggle became noticeable and the cracks in my "outstanding" performance became exposed over time. It was obvious that I wasn't performing to my full potential. That I was distracted. And I struggled to understand my difference was my asset.

New York had been an incredible incubator for five years. It was my safe space as my outward self-exploration eroded the heavy weight I once carried. But New York could only carry me so far. It was now time to discover my passion and fully become me. My New York City graduation date had arrived. It was time to move on.

With an apartment lease ending and the brief, aimless real estate career that I attempted after leaving the stress of Wall Street declining, I opted out of the big city lights on impulse and left for the beach and sunshine of Florida. Even though I had no job lined up and was temporarily staying with a friend, I knew that I needed an environment to relax and to give me time to open up my mind space. A recovery of sorts from living in New York City.

Within a couple weeks after relocating to paradise, a consulting opportunity opened up at a privately owned company headquartered near downtown St. Petersburg. And just like that, I was on my way again, beginning a new chapter.

CORPORATE MASK

A COUPLE YEARS into my consulting gig in Florida, the training department decided that our entire executive team would participate in an assessment that measures each of our most comfortable behaviors and how we naturally prefer to do things. But the most interesting piece of the assessment was that it shows how people modify their style when interacting with different styles of people and in different situations, including when under stress.

After each person had individually taken the assessment, our corporate trainer came in one afternoon several weeks later to walk through the group's results.

The overly enthusiastic woman asked the group of thirty colleagues to stand up in the windowless conference room with awful fluorescent lighting. I could hear the collection of muffled moans as we all stood up and moved our chairs out of the way.

The trainer asked everyone to move to a spot in a large, imaginary circle that took up most of the room. Each quadrant of the circle represented a personal style of how someone operates when outside of the work environment, the more innate style. We all looked down at the individual results printed on the paper that we were holding and slowly shuffled across the worn gray carpet to our spot in the circle. The group started to laugh, seeing the majority of us grouped into the same area.

Next, the trainer asked everyone to move to the quadrant that represented the personal style of how we each operated when we are working in the office environment. By the time I raised my head to begin walking to my new place in the circle, I noticed that most everyone had not moved that far.

The group watched me as I slowly walked to the opposite side of the circle and was the last person to find my spot. The room fell silent, waiting for the trainer to jump in with the key takeaways.

I stood looking back at the group staring at me. Anxiety crawled up my arms, over my shoulders and into my head. The hairs on the back of my neck stood straight out and my face began to turn red. I wanted the trainer to jump in, but it felt like an eternity before she finished flipping pages in the manual she was holding.

"And you can see, Cory must feel like he is putting a mask on when he comes to work each day," the trainer jumped in enthusiastically, obviously proud of the key takeaway for the group. I looked around, thinking I was being filmed for an episode of "Corporate Training Fails."

I swallowed hard, trying not to make any obvious reactions. I had been so great at acting out the corporate closeted gay guy role for years. But on that day, it felt like I had been punched in the gut. And I realized that I had fallen deeper into the corporate closet.

Before this corporate "outing," I had begun to believe it was ok that no one knew my personal life. It had become natural to avoid making friends with people at work so I wouldn't have to engage about non-work-related items. The standard personal greetings showed up in the normal hallway conversations, but I mostly kept to myself. Even after I was promoted and inherited a team of consultants, I kept my distance. But people are naturally curious. They wanted to know all about me, and the mysteriousness that I exuded fueled their curiosity even more.

That moment in our corporate training was like free therapy with an audience: blaring out loud "Cory isn't his true self at work." Up until that point, I had gone through the motions of being closeted at work for so long that it had never occurred to me that I was trying to hide.

Later that evening while driving home, feeling the warm Florida air rushing into my open window, I began reliving the awkward moments that I endured earlier in the day. I imagined myself taking off the tight mask that had been covering my face and setting it down on the passenger seat. How was I supposed to be working at my peak performance when a large portion of my brain was spent trying not to be me?

I AM STILL IN LOVE WITH YOU, BOSS

ALL OF THE team members I had inherited were older than me. Most of them were older by over ten years. However, one of my new team members, Tyler, was close to my age. Tyler was a hyper, yet quirky, guy. He was over six feet tall and had a stocky, linebacker build. Having worked at the company for over ten years, his ambitious, rigidly organized, and impatient personality pushed him to be a top performer within the 200-person company.

A couple of years before I assumed my role as his new manager, Tyler and I realized that we had a mutual friend and occasionally hung out when our friend invited us both out. One hot Saturday evening, Tyler and I attended a house party with our mutual friend. After many cocktails, our friend wanted to go dancing at one of the two gay bars downtown.

A week ago, I had danced the night away with friends at the same bar, but now, after our mutual friend mentioned we should go, hesitation rippled through my once-relaxed body. I didn't want Tyler to know that I was gay since we worked at the same company.

Tyler was standing with a cocktail in his hand next to me and turned his shaved head to get my reaction. I had only known him outside of work for a few months. He knew the same people that I knew at work, so I knew it was risky to put myself in that situation. I was afraid that my personal life would impact my success and forward movement within the company.

Tyler hadn't flinched at all to the proposal and the four vodka sodas that I had consumed over the past hour were kicking in. I shrugged my shoulders and nodded. The three of us jumped into a taxi and arrived at the bar ten minutes later.

"Hey Cory, welcome back," the bartender, Steve, smiled at me when we approached the bar. Tyler could see my entire body freeze and threw his large hand on my shoulder. He gave me a quick "I knew it" smile and said with a reassuring tone, "It's my round. What do you want?"

Even though I was hesitant about Tyler knowing my secret, I knew it was time to begin unlocking the corporate closet. I was becoming too old to continue wearing the corporate mask. Maybe this was my first step to fully being myself in the corporate environment.

Several years after Tyler learned about my sexuality and a year after I became his new manager, we arrived in Columbus, Ohio, for our annual national sales conference. Our entire corporate team traveled to the event to facilitate and engage with the thousands of salespeople we worked with around the country. And each night of the conference turned into a huge booze fest where many of the corporate team members would go out to celebrate and imbibe.

After a fun night of hanging out with a group of people from our corporate team at a karaoke bar, I decided to head back to my hotel room around 1:00 am since I knew the morning would come around and I needed to make sure I was rested. I took off my clothes and lay down on the soft, white sheets that covered the king-sized bed. I pulled up the thick comforter and plugged my phone into the phone charger hanging on my nightstand.

I switched off the light next to my bed and I began to lay back down when I saw my phone light up. It was a text message from Tyler. I clicked on the message to open it up hoping everything was all right.

"Am I wrong? A year and 1/2 after our talk in Tampa and I'm still in love with you. Sorry. I know I'm ugly. I wish I was hot enough. Ugh I hate that you're my boss."

I had been drinking so I didn't know if I had read that correctly. I sat up in my bed, turned the light back on and held the phone back up to reread the text. Shock instantly shot through my fuzzy head.

I ALMOST BECAME ME

Tyler's text took me back to a conversation I had with him several months after he found out that I was gay. We had been drinking at a gay club in Tampa and our mutual friend ended up going home early. After we closed down the club, we walked down the busy street lined with bars to find a taxi back across the bay.

Without any type of lead-in, Tyler told me as we were walking that he had a huge crush on me. It was like a bus came out of nowhere, jumped the curb and plowed into me. My mind exploded just trying to wrap my head around any remote chance that I was interested in dating him. Once I got over that mental hurdle, I tried explaining to Tyler that I was only interested in being a friend to him. And I brought up the obvious fact that we both worked at the same small, conservative, non-diverse company, which created a huge barrier to any type of romantic relationship.

Now three years later in Columbus, it was obvious Tyler hadn't let go of his feelings for me. After my mind began processing the shocking revelations, I quickly sobered up and went into strategy mode. My response had to be genuine and honest without creating a potentially horrible outcome to a friendship.

I let out an annoyed exhale as my tired eyes stared into the bright light coming from the lamp next to my hotel bed. I racked my exhausted brain, trying to find the right response at that time of night. "Dude, relax" was all I could think of. I sent the text, switched the light off and lay back down. Since I had become Tyler's new manager, we had only hung out a few times. I tried to keep my distance, knowing what he had divulged to me that night in Tampa years ago. It would only create unwanted and unneeded awkwardness.

Tyler shot me a text the next morning of the conference, apologizing and realizing what he had done was emotional and due to his drunk state. I felt awkward and confused and felt it was best to avoid running into Tyler the rest of the day. People make drunk mistakes and I realized I needed to move on, forgiving him for this outburst.

Toward the end of the black-tie gala later that evening, marking the end of the national sales conference, I quietly slipped out of the convention center and into the cool, late-summer air. I turned my head to make sure no one saw me escape. I quickly changed into jeans and a t-shirt and met up with local, non-work friends for a fun break away from the past twenty-four hours.

After too many vodka sodas and shots to count, I faintly remember the taxi driver dropping me off in front of my hotel. I tried not stumble as my blurry eyes glanced around the lobby to make sure I didn't see anyone that I knew. After I found my way to my room, I quickly stripped off my clothes and fell into my bed.

Getting up in three hours for the flight home was not going to be fun. But I realized that my phone wasn't plugged into the charger so I reached out my arms from the edge of my bed and pulled out my phone from my jeans pocket. As I plugged the cord into my phone, I noticed a text message from Tyler. My eyes rolled back into my buzzing head. "Oh gosh, what now?"

"Last time I'll say it because I'm going to cry the next four hours. Love you so much and wish I were beautiful enough for you to love me. I've been in love with you for three years. It's not going to happen overnight. Sorry that makes your life tough. Mine has been miserable. Ok, I'm a crying mess. God damn it. And you wonder why I think I'm hideous. If I were attractive, you would like me. Ugh. Sorry. Shutting up cause I can't even see through my tears. See you at 7am."

Without much hesitation and goosebumps forming on my arms, I quickly responded to his shocking message, telling him that we had already talked about this topic a while ago and he knew my thoughts.

"We did. Sorry sorry sorry. Love you Cory. And shutting up now with my pathetic life cause I'm crying too much to type anymore. So sorry that I love you. Ugh," he wrote back. His pain and sorrow was hard to read, yet I felt helpless. I was scared and frightened. I had no idea what to do.

Next thing I knew, my phone began beeping loudly. My head was pounding and the room was still spinning. My tongue felt like sandpaper. When I shut my alarm off, I noticed that Tyler must have texted me after I passed out several hours before.

"Just had to say this one final time: You're smart, brilliant, funny, sexy, and wow, your eyes are the most beautiful I've ever seen. You inspire me and make me want to be a better man. I would love to have been a boyfriend that is the most accepting, supportive, and 100% dedicated to securing our place on top of the world. Together we would have been an unstoppable force to be recognized and reckoned with. I love you, Cory Calvin."

My head hurt too much to think. I threw my phone down on the bed with a disturbed look on my face and jumped into the shower. After quickly jamming all of my clothes into my suitcase, I got dressed in jeans and a long-sleeved t-shirt, put on my dark sunglasses, and met my team in the lobby for our shared ride to the airport.

I wasn't sure if my stomach was grossly turning because I was hungry or because I wanted to throw up or because I was nervous about being in close proximity with Tyler after such a shocking and uncomfortable 36 hours.

No one at the company other than Tyler and one other person knew my secret. And certainly no one knew Tyler's secret. Tyler's actions were certainly grounds for some sort of Human Resources conversation, yet I knew that Tyler's career most likely would be ruined if I said anything. And, deeper than that, his emotional lining could be deeply scarred.

Three months passed since the national sales conference and Tyler and I carried on as we normally had with our working relationship. It was all business. Nothing was ever said again about the awkward situation he had put me in. I made the strategic decision to move forward without addressing the incident, hoping he would realize the severe consequences of continuing any further actions.

Later that fall, Tyler was at a college football game drinking with his fraternity brothers, reminiscing about old times, and he began to text me. I hesitated, but as a friend, I responded, telling him that I thought it was good for him to be around friends since people have noticed he had not been himself at the office.

Immediately playing into what I had feared would happen, Tyler jumped in and used the situation to his advantage. "I promise when I come back, I will put on a better face. And since I can't woo you the normal way, I've started my next film project, which is my love letter to you."

Anger bubbled up inside of me as I looked at my phone screen. Feeling trapped, I knew that I needed to let him know that his messages to me were not ok, but I knew that he needed help, so I carefully crafted a message on my phone. Once I felt good about the message and made sure it was clear, I sent it back to him.

I explained to him that it made more sense to use his creative work to finally come out to himself and to others close to him in his life, and to move beyond me. And that he was setting himself up for failure if he thinks all of his energy spent toward me was going to work. I explained that I came out to myself, my family, and friends over 10 years ago, which freed me from societal captivity. It proved to be a tough process, but once I was finally true to myself, the weight of the world was lifted and allowed me to be who I was born to be.

I wanted to make sure he knew that this coming-out process takes years and that I would never advise dating anyone through that process because the transformation is so emotionally rocky. Tyler had such a long way to go. He needed to focus on being true to himself. He and society in general had held him captive for way too long.

After going through it myself, I am a free human being. Everything has become so clear to me. I know what I want and what I don't want. I explained that I don't want to date an emotionally unstable human being or anyone that has not come out to himself or other people in their lives.

One hour later, the counterattack came in:

"Beautiful Cory, I know who I am and what I want and that's you. Anyone that really matters to me already knows who I am including family and closest friends. And they know how I feel about you. I couldn't care less what anyone else thinks. I'm more in control and stable than you realize even if I've had a tough few days lately. You would know that if you quit running and actually talked to me. And if it would get me a date with you, I'd announce who I am from the rooftops. I'm more interested in earning your trust and feelings and being a partner to you than what the world thinks. Sounds like you still put other people's opinions above your own happiness. I've risked everything from my job to my friendships to tell you how I feel. I'm ready to destroy everything just to get a date with you. You are worth it. Why don't you spend less time projecting who you think I am on me and more time getting to know me?!

"Not to belabor this, just clarifying my tipsy comments. I'm strong as an oak. No plans to 'destroy' anything. Just meant that I don't feel the societal oppression you think I do. But if it will make you feel better, I'll dial every person I know and 'destroy' the phony persona you think I have. I already love myself and know I'm awesome. While my goal is to earn your favor, I am not unstable nor have negative plans or feelings. In fact, I counseled friends all weekend who continuously turn to me for strength. I do plan to continue working professionally as always. If you have any questions let me know. Have a great week."

Tyler's reply made me cringe. Thoughts of him causing me bodily harm would pop up at random times while I was in the office and even when I was at home since he knew where I lived. Workplace shooting stories in the news raced through my mind. Nightmares of him hurting me showed up and I began to lose sleep.

This had gone way too far. After several long days of no response from me, Tyler wrote me back one last time. "OMG this is ridiculous. We have fun when we are together and we want the same things. Can we quit making this so serious and just invest time together?!"

Tyler came to my office right on time for the meeting that I scheduled with him after the long Thanksgiving holiday. My office was on the interior of the building and was lit by horrible, fluorescent lighting from the drop ceiling. Each of the four beige, paper-thin walls were completely bare, and my faux wooden desk faced two uncomfortable metal chairs that sat next to the door. My stomach rolled over as I sat behind my desk in the comfortable, wheeled office chair. I asked Tyler to close the door and it felt like I was going to throw up in my trash can.

Tyler cautiously sat down across from me. He glanced at me, but then would quickly dart his gaze toward the carpeted floor. My voice trembled and I could feel a lump in my throat as I delivered the succinct message that I had rehearsed before Tyler arrived in my office.

With a direct and firm tone, I explained how deeply I had thought about how to handle this situation. I kept my head high and my eyes locked in on him as I concluded by outlining that the next inappropriate, non-business message I receive from him will be taken immediately to our Human Resources department.

Tyler's face was blank and his body remained motionless. I made it clear that our relationship moving forward will be strictly business. I also clarified that his year-end performance review will only be based on his business performance—unless he chose to continue his inappropriate behavior. After a long pause, I asked him if he understood what I had said and if he had any questions.

Tyler nodded and briefly closed his eyes. His defeated body language was tough to watch, but my stern look was unforgiving. He slowly stood up with his notepad in his hand, opened my door, and thanked me like he always had during our routine meetings before walking out.

TIME TO BE ALL OF ME

THE HIRING MANAGER was seated across from me in the small, oval meeting room on the eighth floor of the company's regional headquarters in downtown Chicago. The hour-long interview had gone fairly well, with questions digging into my finance background. The level of the open position was a great fit for an MBA candidate, something I had accomplished a year ago while working full-time in Florida.

I had reached another career plateau with the company in Florida. The business I was a part of was in a dying industry. I had taken the consulting position since it paid well and gave me decent benefits. Florida had given me what I needed after a revved-up beginning to my professional career in New York. The life reset had come at the right moment. But while I was resetting, family turmoil was brewing.

Around the same time that my mother was leaving my father, my sister and her husband ended their relationship. My sister and her one-year-old daughter moved in with my mother. The two main women in my life were now single, yet together. A part of me desired to be physically closer to them. I wanted to be able to drive to see them. It was time to move back to the Midwest.

"Why do you want to work for PepsiCo?" the hiring manager asked. This question, near the end of the interview, deviated in theme from the rest. A large smile appeared on my face as I thought back at how the past ten years of my corporate career had prepared me for this moment.

While I had many reasons to want to work for the company in Chicago, my leading answer was the purest. I proudly told him that it was time to be me. PepsiCo demanded that its employees are different from others. Diversity was at the deep core of the company's values, something I had discovered over a year ago after researching companies that celebrated human and professional differences. I could no longer hide within the corporate closet. It was time to bring my entire self to work, and I knew PepsiCo was the best place for me to blossom.

The hiring manager could see my eyes well up. He could sense my journey had reached a climax and his smile mirrored mine. The unnecessary weight that I had been carrying around about my sexuality in the workplace had been erased in that moment. For the first time in my corporate career, all of me was celebrated.

CHIEF HOMOSEXUAL OFFICER

PEPSICO PROVED A great fit for me. The resources of the Fortune 50 company provided the safe space for me to grow even further as a professional. I noticed that I could fully focus on tasks without having to worry about someone judging me. I knew that my colleagues appreciated me for who I was. This appreciation became the simple, invisible foundation that the environment exuded allowing me to create another powerful self-transformation.

After a year of settling into the company, my self-transformation propelled me to think about how I could help others do what I had done. I fully stepped out of the corporate closet. My productivity improved. I could sense another life purpose begin to appear. And the question I wanted to solve became more and more obvious to me. How could I help others living in the corporate closet become their authentic selves in the workplace?

I thought back through the corporate workspaces I had been a part of and began to see commonalities. While most of the companies had diversity groups, the diversity groups were siloed. The groups only catered to those with visible diversity. It was like the company was just checking a corporate box to have the group and not truly leveraging the purpose of having a diversity group.

For example, African-American groups typically catered to and supported African-Americans. Others could visibly see the diversity. But what about people like me who were in the corporate closet? People like me who were LGBT+ but never saw anyone like them in their company who was out and open and successful. No role models existed. So how do you cater to a diversity that you can't visibly see?

The key question I wanted to answer was, how can companies create role models within the corporate space for those the company may not even know needs them? It became obvious that a visible solution was necessary. People like I had been, living in the corporate closet, needed to see others visibly supporting them.

It wasn't long after I settled into fully being myself at PepsiCo that I became the co-chair of the LGBT+ employee resource group in Chicago. The first project I tackled was creating a corporate program for allies of LGBT+ people to visibly show they are an ally. We called it Ally Day. Since the main part of the program was visibility, we hung posters throughout the office showcasing senior executives with their pictures and quotes outlining why they are an ally. We handed out signs that were hung in employees' work spaces to show others they are an ally. We launched video campaigns showing local employees supporting their LGBT+ employees.

As I stood in front of the large crowd that filled the cafeteria on the first floor, I got the chills seeing almost half of the 1,200 employees in the building had participated in Ally Day.

For the first time in my life I felt deep in my soul that I was making a difference in the lives of others. I only wondered how I could do this type of work full-time instead of what I had been hired to do as a finance manager. It was evident that I loved my gay job more than my day job.

As time went on, I became the co-chair of the global PepsiCo LGBT+ employee resource group. I was the go-to person for anything "gay" in the company. For the month of June, we worked with PepsiCo's CEO to fly the pride flag patterned with our company's logo at our corporate headquarters. Our group helped the company in many ways, which would go on to help many others. I sometimes joked that I had become the Chief Homosexual Officer at PepsiCo.

Global Ally Day went on to become the company's largest-ever employee-led program, expanding into over 30 countries around the world across five continents.

An older woman sought me out at an Ally Day event one year. She placed both of her hands on my shoulders. Tears formed in her eyes as she told me that it was the first time in her twenty-year career that she felt comfortable enough to finally be her full self at work. She had just come out to all of the colleagues at the manufacturing plant she ran as a result of Ally Day. This woman's colleagues welcomed her with open arms. And if it weren't for these allies being visible in their work environment, this woman may never have come out of the corporate closet.

Goosebumps spread across my skin. My eyes watered and I gave her a gigantic embrace, knowing that her life was changed forever. That I had created this moment in her life. I knew in that moment what I wanted to do for the rest of my life. I want to help people who feel they can't do it alone to be able to find out who they were meant to be. To be able to take the mask off and breathe. And to be able to realize their full life potential before their journey ends.

6
SEX

BLACKOUT

MY ENTIRE BODY ached as I opened my eyes. My head was completely numb. As I tried to swallow, my tongue hit the roof of my mouth and it felt like a piece of extremely coarse sandpaper. I wanted to get up out of bed and get some water, but it was as if my body was not connected to my mind. I felt paralyzed.

I pressed my hands down on the bed to attempt to lift up my lethargic frame. But moving quickly reminded me of the ten or so vodka sodas that I consumed last night—and maybe a shot of fireball whiskey, but I wasn't quite sure. As I rolled over on my right side, the air became very stale and I was sure whatever was in my stomach wouldn't remain there long. I wanted nothing else but to remain in the fetal position until this awful feeling went away.

"Why do I do this to myself? Why do I think I need to keep drinking until the bars close?" I thought. "You are getting way too old to do this to your body." It's like I don't want the night to end. "You can do this. You have to get up to get some water and take some ibuprofen so you will begin to feel better."

It took all of my energy, but I managed to push myself up into a seated position. I noticed that my phone lay next to me in bed, but I didn't have the energy to look at it. The light shining into my condo living room filtered over the loft walls of my bedroom and onto the brown, timber ceiling above. I sat for a while as my eyes slowly adjusted to the light. I looked at the nightstand and noticed that my lamp had been turned on all evening.

My clothes were strewn all over the floor below. My jeans lay in a pile near my closet. My black, casual shoes lay randomly on their sides where they had landed after what looked like being tossed. My black socks balled up next to my shoes like they had been quickly stripped off. And my green t-shirt was bunched up near my nightstand.

I managed to put my feet on the cold, wooden floor one at a time and sat at the edge of my bed. Dull pains shifted around in my head, reminding me of what I did to my body only about eight hours prior. The room began to awkwardly spin as the blood rushed from my head as I stood up. Every movement seemed like the most difficult movement I had ever had to make.

I clumsily walked around my bed, holding my hand up over the gray comforter covering my bed to maintain my balance. I staggered into the hallway toward the kitchen supporting myself on each side by the light gray walls. The mid-morning sunlight pierced through the floor-to-ceiling windows in the living room.

The warm, stagnant air hit my face. And I could hear the light buzz of the cars speeding by along the highway just outside my condo building. I turned the corner, entered my kitchen and noticed a white cardboard box on my kitchen island. I opened the box and the smell of cold pizza wafted up at me.

My stomach rolled over as my cheeks puffed out, thinking my stomach was about to empty itself all over the granite countertop. Only one of the two slices had been eaten. It was a mystery to me when I stopped to get pizza the night before or how I even got home.

My body was screaming, "Get water now!" I opened the wooden cabinet beside my refrigerator and sorted through the small white plastic bottles. I pulled out the ibuprofen and violently snapped open the cap. The pills almost flew everywhere. I shook three softgels into the palm of my left hand and then threw the pills into my mouth.

I could taste the generic plastic taste of the softgels as they stuck to the side of my mouth. I pulled open the refrigerator, picked up the large Brita container and set it on the countertop. I opened up the cabinet to pull out a glass and then filled it up with cold water.

The cold water flowed down my throat like water gushing down a waterslide. The small bumps on my tongue began to go away as the water cleaned out the dryness that had formed in my sleep. A wave of energy pulsated through my system that felt like I had plugged myself into a power source to recharge my body.

I emptied the full glass of water and then refilled it for a second round.

I swallowed the entire glass with one gulp and then released a giant exhale, appreciating what I had just done. After setting the glass down, I placed both hands down on the countertop to take a rest. I looked out at the freeway below and began laughing out loud. "You crazy party animal," I said to myself, shaking my head. And then I began to wonder what really did happen last night.

After chugging another glass of water, I managed to walk back to my room to find my phone. The battery was nearly dead and about to turn off, so I plugged it into the power cord. All of this activity had exhausted me, so I gently sat down on my bed. There was no way I could hold myself up, so I lay back down onto my soft pillows.

CRAIGSLIST AD

IT FREAKS ME out when I can't remember details about the night before. I looked at the photos on my phone to see if that would help me remember anything, but nothing was there. Then I figured that if I took an Uber, I probably received an email receipt showing what time I arrived home.

I opened up my email app and noticed that I had 54 new messages. I have never had that many messages over the course of one night. But as I opened up my email app, I noticed that 49 of the 54 messages were for an email account that I rarely use. In fact, it is an email account that I had set up when I had first moved to New York City in 2001 primarily for discreetly meeting other guys so I could remain completely anonymous.

It allowed me to randomly communicate with others without having to use my normal email account with my name attached to it. I created a random name so no one would know who I was.

I immediately sat up in bed as my eyes almost popped out of my head. The quick motion made my stomach turn, as it was a bad reminder never to drink that much again. What happened last night? My mind was racing. Why would I have 49 new messages since yesterday evening on an email account I hadn't used in years?

My head was still pounding as I opened up the email account and saw all of the new messages stacked on top of each other. It instantly felt like someone had punched me in the gut. The subject line for all of the messages was a reply to a Craigslist personal ad.

I stared at my screen and I could feel the vodka and sodas stirring in my stomach. Beads of sweat formed on my forehead and my palms turned damp. I didn't know whether to laugh hysterically or to berate myself. I thought my New York City phase of my life, when I would cruise online for a one-night stand, was over.

I tried so hard to think of anything that would trigger my mind into remembering anything that happened between leaving the bar and passing out in my bed. If I didn't remember anything, how was I able to write up an advertisement that was legible enough to post online to Craigslist?

Facetiously, I thought it was a little impressive to be able to do all of that and not even remember what happened when I woke up in the morning. I shook my head in disbelief. And, I thought, what kind of person responds to Craigslist ads anymore? But then even more embarrassing, I thought, who *writes* Craigslist personal ads anymore?

My ceiling fan was on high, blowing air toward my sweaty face as I lay there staring at my phone screen. My finger pulled the screen up as I scrolled through the messages. I still couldn't believe forty-nine people took the time to read my posting between the hours of two and ten in the morning and spend the energy to send me a message. What had I done?

In that moment of flicking through the emails on my phone, it hit me. The ad was still live. I scrolled to the bottom of the emails and found the confirmation email. I clicked the link to the live ad and there it was in all its glory. *"MUSCULAR HAIRY STUD LOOKING FOR FUN"*

I read the very specific and descriptive ad that I somehow managed to coherently type. My eyes almost popped out of my head as I continued to scroll down. There it was: a headless, shirtless photo of my torso. "OH MY GOSH" I yelled out loud. I left nothing for the imagination. A slow deep giggle escaped my mouth as I shook my head. With a half grin on my face, I removed the live posting.

I reached over and gently placed my phone back on the night-stand. The only thing that I planned was to meet Luke, a guy I had met a few weeks ago online, for a second date in a park later in the afternoon. I pulled my feather pillow up under my ear and adjusted my head a couple times to get comfortable. Now that I was able to figure out what had happened last night, I could shut my eyes and try to get this headache to go away.

But as I lay there listening to the fan spin around, my mind wouldn't stop. Two conflicting voices in my head battled it out. One side remembered the unsatisfied, guilty, empty feelings I would have after a hookup, throwing me into a state of depression. The other side of my mind wanted a quick fix as a replacement for intimacy to overcome my insecurities.

I reached out my arm, now feeling a sense of commitment. To just go for it and give in to my insecurity. I rolled onto my back and unlocked my phone. There they were. All of the messages stacked on top of each other staring me right in the face.

My index finger clicked on the first message sent at 2:04am. Oh. My. Gosh. My hand smacked down over my face. Utter shock and embarrassment whipped through my mind as I began reading through the messages. Photos of shirtless torsos. Descriptions of what the respondents wanted to do sexually. Some guys even seemed genuine and put a lot of thought into their reply.

Once I read a message, I flipped quickly to another, curious of what people sent. My stomach churned when I read how several guys shared that they had girlfriends or had children and needed to remain discreet. I couldn't stop reading, but I began to feel ashamed that I had created all of this.

After flipping through about twenty messages and immediately deleting each message after reading, my eyes became transfixed on the photo that a guy named 'Ryan' included in his response. Received at 6:44am, the photo showed his arm holding the camera and his bicep bulging like a huge rock was shoved under his t-shirt sleeve. A light layering of brown body hair covered his sculpted pectoral muscles. And each abdominal muscle popped out of his stomach. As my eyes continued down his midsection, I could see the creases in his skin where his legs met his torso. Each line angled downward, forming the letter V.

A thin layer of moisture formed on my arms as I lightly touched my neck and then my upper chest. My heartbeat increased and my breathing became shallower. My body became warm with excitement.

Conflicted, I thought that seeing Ryan's email was exactly why I should have just deleted everything and not have read any of the emails. I laid my phone down, trying to stop the momentum that I had just created. But I couldn't get his photo out of my mind.

We all have moments in life where a decision to do something or not to do something lead down two very different paths. One of those paths will become reality and the other will be an unwritten story. Do I respond to Ryan, or do I just delete the email and write it off as a funny story that I will write in a book one day?

But it was too late. My mind raced with excitement as lay in my bed. I had already gone down a path of no return. Five hours had passed since Ryan initially wrote me. But after some initial hesitation, I wrote back, *"Hot pic man. Face pic?"*

I continued reading the remaining emails after I inexcusably sent my reply. I pulled my finger down to refresh the inbox on my phone and I noticed that Ryan replied to my note. Attached was a pic of his very handsome face. His perfectly white teeth were grinning widely, stretching his lightly bearded cheeks to the side. My heart fluttered as I wondered if this guy was for real. I felt like I had won the lottery for sexiest man alive. While my heart wanted to believe he was real, the other part of me doubted if the person on the other end was truthful.

I couldn't stop myself. With each note from Ryan, I felt like I had to send a reply back. Over the next two hours, Ryan and I exchanged emails about potentially meeting later that day. He was flying in to visit friends and asked if he could stop by after he landed. I realized that I created a drunken ad looking for fun, and the voices inside my head were telling me to stop replying. I didn't want to endure the guilt and depression from putting myself in that situation again.

THE GREEK STALLION

I WAS SO fixated on emailing Ryan that I had forgotten about my date with Luke was coming up in thirty minutes. The sunlight poured through my windshield when I pulled out of the damp underground parking garage and I sent Luke a text message letting him know I was running behind.

Luke and I met on Tinder. He had barely written anything in his profile, but his rugged face, thick facial hair, defined cheeks, and rigid jawline made me swipe right.

For our first date, we met at a great Italian restaurant in Andersonville, a Chicago neighborhood sort of halfway between where we both lived. Luke could have been a collegiate football player. He stood a full six foot two with broad shoulders. He oozed sexy as his pecs and his arms bulged out of his t-shirt that must have been a size too small. His short, dark-brown hair connected into his dark, five o'clock shadow.

The smell of tomato sauce entered my nose as I walked into the restaurant for our first date. And Luke's huge grin lit up the room as he wrapped his massive arms around me. A very sweet embrace for a first meeting, even though he about crushed me with the powerful squeeze. But I could feel my body heating up, feeling his solid chest and midsection pushing up against mine. Pent-up nervousness instantly escaped my body as a result of touching his.

"How was your day?" I asked, trying to kick off our initial meeting in a light way that would allow us to ease into a more meaningful "getting to know you" conversation. Luke began to tell me about his day and the sound of his deep, masculine voice with his sexy Greek accent made me think that I could listen to him all day.

"Do you live on your own?" I asked when he began telling me about where he lived.

"No, I have two roommates. But it is a duplex. I have my own living space on the bottom floor and they have their own living space on the upper floor," Luke responded.

"That is nice to have your own full living space. So are your roommates your friends or just people that you find to rent out the place?" I continued.

"Well, actually they are my relatives," Luke said as he sat back in the booth like he was uncomfortable. He looked away from me. I didn't really know where he was going with this conversation. I thought to myself that he must live with cousins or some close relatives.

"They are my parents," he said, as he could tell I looked confused.

"Oh," I said in a way that tried to hide my disbelief. But my eyes must have gotten larger and my eyebrows must have raised. My mind went spinning as I was trying to find the right thing to say. But any response I had wouldn't stick. I tried to envision a 44-year-old man living with his parents. Sure, he explained the living areas were different, but I couldn't get it out of my head that he lived with his parents.

My thoughts controlled my facial expressions. Luke could see the look of shock on my face. It was like the dating referee quickly ran over to our table and threw down the red flag. After a split second of disappointment, I tried to quickly overlook the unexpected piece of information and attempted to engage.

But once the red flag was released, it was like I began a scavenger hunt to find more. As the conversation continued, I wasn't able to recover. I continued asking him questions to get to know him further, but red flags kept appearing. One after another. It became apparent that Luke didn't have much in his conversational repertoire other than past dating experiences, gym workouts, nutritional supplements, and his personal training clients. The meathead stereotype kept playing over and over and over as he spoke.

The experience sort of reminded me of a date I went on when I lived in St. Petersburg, Florida. The guy lived on a peacock farm and showed up to the date an hour late with bandages on his fingers saying he bit them too hard on a recent late-night drive to go out to clubs in Miami so he wouldn't fall asleep since he has narcolepsy.

Red flags flew left and right on my date with Luke. Another first date disaster. But the grand finale came when Luke shared that his parents didn't know that he was gay. I should have just gotten up and left after hearing this admission. But ditching someone is not my style. He is a person with feelings, so I will show my respect and will just chalk up the experience as dating practice.

I'd already decided my date with Luke was a one-and-done date, like many other dates I have had in my lifetime. Sure, this guy was a Greek stallion, but sexy was his only asset. The external Luke was oozing hotness. But the internal Luke was oozing molasses on a cold winter day.

Before I had time to think of something to deflect the disappointing ending after we had stepped outside, Luke said, "I had such a great time. And I would love to hang out again. How about next Sunday in the afternoon? If it's nice we can go to the park."

Luke's naive inquiry came out of nowhere. BAM! "That sounds nice," I replied so quickly that I didn't even know what had happened. I had unexpectedly committed to a second date as my body was immediately squeezed by muscle hotness. This grand finale was a huge distraction to what I was really thinking.

The divergent feelings about our first date was still fresh on my mind as I sped through city traffic to my second date with Luke. "Why didn't you just tell him you weren't interested in moving forward? Why couldn't you just be honest with him?" I thought. Rejection sucks for sure. But I am sure no one wants to be dragged along only to be told 'no' later. My stomach knotted, realizing the situation that I had put us both in. It wasn't fair to him. I felt dishonest.

WIN-WIN

AFTER WHAT SEEMED like twenty minutes of driving around, I finally found a parking spot on the street several blocks from the park. I was twenty minutes late for my second date with Luke, but I wasn't upset about it.

The trees were budding. The fresh smell of flowers infused into the late-spring air as I walked along the cracked concrete side-walk. Luke's radiant smile appeared when I turned the corner to the historic stone archway that marked the park entrance. I could hear the screams and laughter of young children playing on the playground near the entrance. Parents sat around next to their empty strollers and looked on as the controlled chaos played out in front of them.

Luke's manly figure was adorable as he stood there in a tight white t-shirt and form-fitting blue jeans. His outstretched arms were like a giant, sexy landing pad waiting for me to touch down and stay a while. However, resistance flowed throughout my body as I continued toward him. I flashed up a cheeky smile as I got closer. And... touchdown. His thick arms devoured my body and the smell of his powerful cologne that must have been bought at one of those cheap perfume stores violated my nostrils.

After he released me from his mega-hold, we exchanged small talk as we began a slow, steady stroll through the park. It was difficult for me to erase the conversation from our first date. But this fact reminded me to be as honest as I could on this outing. The intellectual and emotional pieces I need from someone were both absent. It was only fair to politely tell him that I wasn't interested in a third date—one of the worst parts of dating.

"I was out so late last night. I don't know why I do that to myself at this age. I know that I will feel like crap the next day, like I do now. I woke up this morning and barely remembered how I got home last night," I explained after Luke asked me how my weekend was going.

And as I continued chatting with Luke, Ryan's emails from earlier that day popped into my head. Guilty feelings rushed through me for having thoughts about a guy while on a date with someone else.

Instinctually, I reached into my jean's pocket to pull out my phone and check my messages. But as my phone was halfway out, reality snapped me back. I was on a date with Luke. Don't be rude. Focus on Luke.

I continued telling him about my weekend. Luke shared about his weekend and how some of his personal training clients didn't show. He was trying out a new supplement to give his already bulging muscles a boost.

Luke continued talking about protein and free weights and physical therapy as I began to feel anxious. The shadows from the trees had shifted and I realized we had been sitting on the wooden park bench longer than I expected. I anxiously wanted to check my phone because I was certain Ryan had landed. And I knew I needed to rip the Band-aid off. It was time for the dreaded date moment.

"Luke, it was really nice to hang out again. I had a nice time. And I need to get going," I began, once there was a logical break in the conversation. "I would like to remain friends with you."

"Great, so you want to hang out again?" Luke responded, but I could tell he wasn't catching on to my indirect way of saying I don't want to go on another date with him.

My muscles tensed and I felt myself becoming impatient. After a short pause, I responded, "Actually, I think it makes the most sense to be friends." His grin lowered and his eyes drooped. Disappointment overwhelmed his face. But the worst moment of dating has to happen if it isn't a match.

"He will be better off. I will be better off. It's a win-win. This is the best thing for the situation," my mind produced as I tried to stay firm with what I said and not break into banter. "Ok, now it's time to hug him and leave. No need for more chit chat to make it worse..."

With my lips pressing together, I tilted my head and softened my eyes. I opened up my arms and wrapped them around his strong frame. His body tightened up, protecting himself.

"It was really nice to get to meet you and get to know you. I'm sure our paths will cross again soon," I said lightly into his ear as we were still in a lingering embrace. I released my arms and backed away. I looked into his eyes, trying to tell him with my expression that I was sorry but this will all work out the way it's supposed to.

His head angled toward the ground and his shoulders pulled forward. As I turned away, my eyes focused on the large stone archway up ahead and I took each sad step to exit the park. I thought to myself how it is interesting how something so difficult in life only lasts about two to three minutes. But having the courage to be honest is the part that takes the most energy.

THE MEETING

ONCE I WAS out of sight from the park, I reached into my jeans pocket and pulled out my phone with anticipation. I could feel the adrenaline working its way through my mind, my chest, my pelvis and hips. And there it was. Several text messages from a random number I had not seen before.

"I've been waiting at the train station. I will wait a little longer before I need to go. Do you still want to meet?" My eyes fixated on the message. I couldn't believe he actually texted me. I glanced up at the time at the top of my phone, noticing that it was 6:03pm. "Crap. I wonder if he is still waiting," I thought to myself.

The entire situation was so anticlimactic. Anxiously waiting for his text message all day, receiving the message, and then feeling that all I wanted was to be alone. I had no mental energy to handle all of this right now. Only minutes before, images of Ryan raced through my mind, but now images of Luke's dejected face were front and center. My head began to throb a little. Maybe I shouldn't respond to the message, I thought.

My mental capacity was depleted. But then I knew that not responding to Ryan would make him feel rejected. It was like the theme of the day. Rejection to the other 48 people that I never responded to, to Luke, and then to Ryan. And then, finally, to me.

Endorphins in my body were non-existent. Serotonin levels depleted. I had set myself up for this depressed state twenty-four hours ago with feelings of loneliness and sadness before going out drinking with my friends and hoping that going out would help ease some of the sadness. Dancing, laughter, and chatting with friends was great. But the alcohol mixed with an environment of emptiness at the gay bar created mild depression.

"Hey, sorry, my lunch with a friend lasted much longer than I thought. I'm on my way back home. But are you sure you want to come over?" I wrote back to him, thinking that I could try to push him away instead of ignoring him altogether. I felt bad that this guy had built up anticipation all day to meet up with me, traveled some sort of distance by flight, and was now waiting at a train station anticipating my reply.

"It's not a problem, man. I can come over for a little while to help you out. Where should I go?" he immediately wrote back.

"You have your luggage with you. It's annoying to lug all of that on the train, man," I continued, to try to get him to give up.

"If you don't want me to come over, just tell me. I've waited here for the past twenty minutes to hear from you. I don't mind taking the train. It's fine for me," he threw back, keeping me honest.

I could see the entire thing playing out in my head. He comes over. We get off. He leaves an hour later. And I am annoyed that I had him over when I could have taken care of myself in five minutes without all the hassle of having someone over. Then I could just make dinner and go to bed early, catching up on some sleep I lost from the night before. And once he leaves, I will feel that I let myself down again, fueling further feelings of inner sadness.

But I couldn't get the image out of my head of him standing on the train station platform all alone waiting for me. "What the hell, Cory. Just help him out. He has come a long way to make this work," my mind produced.

"No, you can come over. I was just trying to prevent you from going through all that hassle. Take the blue line toward Forest Park and get off at the Racine stop. When you get off the train, text me and I will tell you how to find me."

"Sweet. I am on my way," he wrote back.

I started up my car and plugged my phone into my car charger. I opened up Waze to find the fastest way home. I had committed. Everything that Ryan and I discussed via email was about to happen.

As I was pulling into my parking spot in the damp, underground parking garage connected to my building, Ryan texted me saying he was at the Racine stop, which was just a block away from my condo. All he needed to do was walk up the ramp, cross the bridge and then turn to come to my building.

I sent Ryan the quick route to my building as I walked into the freight elevator to head up to my place. I hurried into my condo, quickly made up my bed and threw all of my clothes that were cluttered on the floor into my clothes hamper.

"I'm here. Come down and let me in boss," he wrote me back several minutes later. I was confused. No one ever wants me to go down to get them. I usually just have the guy dial up and I unlock the building entrance by hitting a button. What if someone in my building saw me let him in? They would immediately realize that

I had invited someone over to hook up. Or they would wonder why I didn't just buzz up a friend.

Maybe he was different. Even though I had no intention of kissing him, I decided to quickly brush my teeth in case my breath smelled bad. I thought to myself how I tell people I don't want to kiss during a hookup. It is way too intimate for me. Kissing is almost more intimate than the act of making love. It can create a strong emotional connection very quickly. And since the person is just over to my place for a casual encounter, I don't want to get attached. It's like I have taught myself to compartmentalize emotions and romance separate from the physical act of sex.

Thinking that I had to make a hot first impression, I changed my shirt to a cut off t-shirt to show off my toned arms. I put on some gym shorts that were easy to take off. Grabbing my keys and phone from the bench seated next to the door, I hurried out. I locked the deadbolt even though I wasn't going to be gone for very long and walked down the hallway. The hallway was dimly lit, but I could see the horizontal timber beams along the ceiling. My flip flops clicked against the carpeted floor as I made my way to the elevator at the front of the building.

As I headed down, I rolled through my mental checklist. Remember to smile. Remember to stay calm and avoid showing how nervous you are. Remember to just be you. Remember to not let this linger forever. Just get the deed done and then make dinner so you can have an early night.

The elevator doors slid open and I threw a quick grin on my face. I looked straight ahead through the security door that led out to the small lobby. But I could not see anyone. I took a couple steps to the first security door and pushed the security latch to open the door.

As I pushed open the interior glass door, sunlight entered through the thick panes of the lobby's side door around the corner. My eyes quickly adjusted and I first noticed his lime green t-shirt that snugly fit a very broad, muscled frame. My focus shifted upwards to this huge, brilliant smile aimed directly at me. And then our brown eyes locked. His brown hair was perfectly parted and pulled over to his right side. His dark beard was trimmed and I could tell he had just shaved earlier that day, cleaning up the neatly lined edges.

There he stood holding his small, black suitcase on wheels outside of the exterior security door. He couldn't stop smiling as his body nervously extended as tall as it could. By now my smile mirrored his. It was like time slowed down and our energy pulsated between us.

I reached for the latch and proceeded to open the door. Ryan pulled the exterior door handle and walked around the open door with a wide grin stuck on his face.

"Hey, glad you found it," was the first thing that blurted out of my dry mouth. "I tried to tell you it was a pain."

He was quickly chomping away at a piece of green gum that matched the color of his shirt. "I can't believe I ended up on the pink line," he said with a deep chuckle acknowledging he unexpectedly took the wrong train line. His voice had a sexy, masculine tone but I could hear a slight, nervous quiver as he spoke.

He walked into the first door and I unlocked the second security door with my key fob. Once I pressed the elevator button, the doors immediately opened since I had just taken the ride down to the first floor and we walked in. We stood close to each other, face to face, with his bag between us as the elevator began to lift up. I occasionally glanced over his head, sizing him up, since he was about six inches shorter than I was.

The awkward moment of first meeting someone and knowing what was about to happen but not knowing what to say to each other had begun. "Thanks for coming all this way. Honestly, I didn't think you would show up. People online are usually fake and since you were coming from so far, I didn't put much on you actually following through," I said to break the awkward silence, knowing that in a matter of minutes we probably would be naked on my bed.

"I'm not your typical online guy. You could be a liar or a fake also. That is why I had you come down to get me. If you would have been 400 pounds or didn't match your picture I would have just left," he said with another nervous giggle.

"Oh I get it. I mean I could have been a serial killer or some crazy person. I still could be," I said, laughing a little, but it made the banter a little awkward because it was believable. The elevator doors opened and Ryan walked out with his bag. I pulled open the main door to the fourth-floor hallway and he followed behind me, wheeling his bag along the carpet.

"So, what is your real name?" I asked as I turned around with a big grin on my face.

He let out a deep laugh, realizing that I knew the drill. "It's Craig, what's yours?"

"Awesome to meet you in person Craig." I exhaled like I just made an important discovery. "Ahhh, so *you* are the owner of Craigslist?" We both laughed out loud for second time in the quiet hallway.

This feeling of warmth washed over me as I looked back at him. My heart was still tingling. My entire body felt light, like my brain's energy was circulating love throughout my body. I had never felt this way before.

Up until this point in my life I did not believe in love at first sight. But was this love at first sight? Was I actually falling in love with him? I started to question if I wanted to hook up with him. I wanted to get naked with him for sure, but I felt that I wanted to get to know him first. To court him. To have a first kiss. To ease into intimacy. To build a foundation of a relationship instead of just jumping into the sack to experience sex before even knowing his last name.

"He is the one," popped into my head. I felt an immediate connection to him. Like I had known him for years. It felt so comfortable to be in his presence. The romantic in me wanted to just slow things down. But how would I do that, when what was about to happen was set into motion many hours prior to this moment? The momentum had built up quickly and it would be almost impossible to pause.

FLOW OF ECSTASY

AFTER ALL OF the build-up in my mind, I decided that I didn't want to have sex with Craig. I wanted to just get to know him with his clothes on. To look into those beautiful brown eyes and learn all about him. It was obvious that I would approve what was underneath those clothes. He was certainly dating material and not some sleazy hookup.

We arrived at my condo and I slid the key into the keyhole to unlock my door. He followed me into the place where only hours earlier, with many miles between us, I had been messaging him. And now he was standing in my foyer. He set his bag down with the handle still pulled up.

"I need to use your bathroom, boss," he said as he had located the bathroom with his eyes and just proceeded to go in. It was a little odd that he didn't ask me, but I just said ok. I thought about walking out into my kitchen at the front of my place so he could just meet me out there and we could begin talking. But then I thought that I didn't want him to get confused when he came out of the bathroom so I just stood at the edge of my bed in my room, which was right next to the bathroom. He would certainly see me when he was finished.

I could hear the stream of urine hit the water in the toilet bowl as he was standing there with the door cracked. The faucet turned on in the sink as he was washing his hands. I stood in silence, wondering again if I should have gone out to the kitchen so there would be no temptation to just rip each other's clothes off in my bedroom. But it was too late. He dried his hands with the towel next to the sink, shut off the light, and opened the door.

As he walked out of the bathroom, he turned and noticed me standing there. Light filtered into my bedroom from the dim foyer combined with some daylight over the loft walls. Our eyes locked. His body moved closer to my body until he stood directly in front of me.

Our eyes sent the same energy back and forth that we experienced downstairs when I let him into the building. We did not know exactly what the energy was, but we could feel the passion vibrating between our souls. Almost like our souls became instantly connected.

I reached my arm out and placed it gently on his pec because I couldn't hold myself back any longer from feeling the massive hunk of muscle. His arm raised and mirrored my movement. The childhood game 'Simon Says' popped into my mind. You do, then I do.

His touch raised goosebumps along my arms and chest. My skin cooled as though his energy instantly combined with mine.

I reached out my other hand and placed it on his shoulder. Our eyes both open and locked on the other's. It was like a force greater than I could control pulled my head closer to his face. There was nothing I could do now to stop the momentum. My eyes slightly closed as my lips lightly pressed onto his.

A colossal collision of pent-up energy erupted as our lips stayed connected. His sculpted body pressed into mine as my arms wrapped completely around his body. It was like it was a puzzle piece that perfectly fit. Our eyes were shut and our hearts were both beating faster as we could feel the deep connection between us.

The kisses became deeper and much more intense. As the intensity picked up, it felt as though our grip on each other became tighter. Like we wanted to pull ourselves into the other person's body. Like our bodies were becoming one.

An indescribable force swarmed around our intertwined bodies and transported us to a fantasy world. A place where time stood still. A magical moment with no beginning and no end. This was different than I had ever experienced.

I could feel my tear ducts beginning to turn on. But I didn't care. I had become the most present that I had ever been. I surrendered my entire being. Our hands began to freely explore each other's entire back, rubbing and caressing over the fabric of our t-shirts.

All of our mental and emotional barriers had been cleansed and purified. The thoughts and feelings from the past twenty-four hours became afterthoughts. Our bodies and our minds had become free and open to endless possibilities.

I opened my eyes halfway and saw Craig's dark eyes looking directly at me. Our lips slowly began to peel away as his lusty eyes told me he was right where he needed to be. He glanced down and grabbed the hem of my t-shirt.

His hands slowly began to lift my white shirt upward, exposing my bare stomach. With a smug grin, I carefully lifted my arms toward the timber ceiling, ready for the moment to continue. Craig gently let go of my shirt as it dropped to the floor.

I smiled and repeated the same for him. As I slowly lifted his shirt over his head, I could see the curves on his body that his muscles had created. First his hairy pectoral muscles that had caught my attention in the first photo. And his thick arms appeared as the t-shirt sleeves pulled away. I dropped his shirt next to mine as we stood face to face at the edge of my bed.

Craig gently grabbed both of my shoulders and turned me so my back was facing the full length of the bed. He stood in front of me looking at me the entire time with this cheeky, playful grin on his face. His hands moved down to my hairy chest as I tried to anticipate what would happen next.

Craig's hands pressed into my body as he gave me a firm but gentle push into my chest. With no resistance, my tall frame fell backward and I landed on the soft, dark gray comforter. Craig lifted his knees onto the bed and I could hear his shoes hitting the floor. I kicked off my flip flops as Craig positioned himself, straddling over my midsection.

My arms lay outstretched on the bed above my head with my body fully surrendered. I looked up and could see his beautifully built pectoral muscles squeezed together like he was a bust sculpture in a museum perched up on top of me. His huge grin was enough for me to feel like this was all a dream. That I was going to wake up tomorrow morning and wonder where he was. This couldn't be reality.

"Now, what am I going to do with you, boss?" he eventually said after staring down at me for several seconds.

"Whatever you want to do to me, boss," I quickly answered in a hopelessly romantic way. The kind of response I had been dreaming about for years.

His shirtless body collapsed onto mine. The soft hair on his chest and stomach pressed down against my furry upper torso. It was pure man on man. Masculinity touching masculinity. Human touching human. Heart touching heart. Soul touching soul.

Craig's deep kisses were enough to make me melt into the bed. And at that moment we entered a flow of ecstasy that lasted for the next hour and a half. I never wanted this moment to end. I would remember this moment for the rest of my life.

7
RED FLAGS

THE COMING OUT STORY

THE SMELL OF grease throughout the restaurant made my mouth water. I could almost taste the juicy cheeseburgers that I had heard so much about as we waited for our table. The wait was over two hours, but I had stopped by the famous restaurant to put in a reservation before I picked Craig up at the train station. After dropping his bag off at my place, we had enough time to enjoy our slow, casual walk to restaurant row in the West Loop.

The small, narrow bar was filled with groups waiting for one of the few tables in the back. As I sipped on my perfectly hand-crafted Old Fashioned, my eyes glowed in disbelief that he was sitting in front of me. It had only been five days since I dropped him off at the train station the morning after one of the most inconceivable nights that I had ever experienced, thinking that it would be the last time I would ever see him again. Like a unicorn you only see once in your dreams.

The past five days had been a downward spiral of emotions. I was unable to drag myself out of bed for the ensuing forty-eight hours after I met Craig. I curled up in my bed, thinking back through every second of my overnight encounter with him. One minute I smiled with pure delight and elation and the next my stomach would churn with anxiety. I wanted him so badly, yet my mind schizophrenically designed future scenarios that ran rampant in my head. Scenarios that shifted into depressing and negative outcomes. My self-imposed confusion spiraled into tears and a feeling of emptiness.

Now, our effortless banter at the bar filled my soul with joy and hope and seemed to instantly relinquish all of the fear I had fabricated only days earlier. My face oozed excitement. I was almost giddy with anticipation about the next few hours. I hadn't ever felt this way about a date. My mind raced with all of the first date questions that I couldn't wait to infuse into the conversation once we settled into our table. I wanted to know everything about him. What made him tick. What his quirks were. What his family was like. Everything.

The hostess sat us at a square table nestled in the corner. The table closest to ours was a comfortable distance away, giving us the freedom to open up a bit more about ourselves. It was perfect for our first "official" date.

As we sat down, the anticipation amplified. The warm light from the candle on the table flickered onto his soft face. He flashed his million-dollar smile and my skin began to tingle. His confident, strong build stimulated my lust. We explored the menu together, discussing the options and the possibility of potentially sharing certain foods. As I continued to savor the moment, I sensed his nerves were activated, stiffening up his shoulders and back.

The thoughts of our conversations during the night that we met flashed through my mind. I remembered that he lived in Philadelphia. And even though I had created a no-long-distance dating rule for myself, I thought how easy it would be to make an exception for Craig.

Butterflies began to flutter. He exuded so much mystery. Just days ago, I didn't know if I would see him again and now he was sitting in front of me. Just the two of us.

The low-lit atmosphere buzzed with energy and the conversation began to deepen. It was like fireworks were going off around us as we kept chatting and continuing to learn what we had in common. Like a dream come true, everything kept getting better as we got to know more about each other.

At one point, Craig and I burst out into laughter talking about how we met. Embarrassed and still somewhat shocked, we both agreed that no one could ever know about that fateful day. And even though it was unspoken, we knew a reason must have existed to put us together like that. Something we held in our hearts as a special bond.

As we continued enjoying our conversation, Craig casually revealed that this dinner was the first time that he had gone on a date with a guy. An odd feeling overtook me, like the loud music playing in the background had suddenly skipped a beat. Instantly caught off guard, my mind reeled through the questions that I had pre-planned in an effort to figure out what I had just heard.

"So when did you come out?" I carefully asked, knowing this would reveal a lot about him. This question typically leads to the "right of passage" story that most LGBT+ individuals share. A story about the intimate moments with family members or friends that can be vividly recounted like it happened yesterday because the energy leading up to that point usually was extremely monumental.

Craig surreptitiously gazed down at the warm candlelight gently dancing through the clear glass holder. His uncanny pause sent a shiver through my shoulders and down through my spine. After a long moment, his eyes met mine.

"I'm currently married to a woman," he softly said. My heart skipped several beats and it began to feel like someone had just poked thousands of needles into my skin. My body froze and it became difficult to swallow. The shifting candlelight reflected in his glassy eyeballs. One side of his mouth curled up in a nervous flinch. All of the excitement and hours of anticipation instantly escaped my mind as disappointment, fear, sadness, confusion, and frustration replaced them.

One simple phrase had paralyzed my heart and mind. After a long awkward moment of gazing into each other's eyes, he could sense my shock and continued on with his story. He and his wife had been married for three years, but they had been separated and living apart for the past year. They had no children and this was his first marriage.

My glorious plan of getting to know him abruptly shifted down an unforeseen path. I knew that I wanted to know everything about what I had just heard. But it quickly became apparent that he had many things going on inside of his mind and also inside of his heart. As he spoke, only small, superficial facts came out. Only divulging the minimum to satisfy any questions that I had. His emotions were tightly locked up behind the very thick wall that he had built. The key to any opening to get through that thick wall was certainly lost.

Since he had been separated from his wife, he had two other encounters with men that he also met online. And those were the only two experiences that he had ever had with men. I felt like I was frozen in time and couldn't move as the words awkwardly stumbled out of his numb mouth.

"So does anyone in your life know about any of this?" I nervously asked, almost shielding myself from the answer.

"I guess one person now," he responded with a nervous giggle. My half smile didn't really sell how I was feeling as thoughts of my long, emotional coming out process began to creep into my mind's eye. All of the painful moments trying to make sense of the feelings that I was having with no one to speak with. And then imagining layering all those feelings over my life at 35 years old. I couldn't quite wrap my head around how it would feel to re-explore my sexuality at this point in my life.

Moment by moment my heart began to crumble. Why was I experiencing this moment? It was like my gut had been right all along as it spoke to me last week. Like I had known this was going to happen.

I should have stood up and walked away. But I was captured by his spell. I wasn't able to give up that quickly. Even though my practical brain observed vast emotional unrest lodged deep within his soul, my hopeful heart felt something pure about him. He hadn't been living the gay life like I had for the past fifteen years. He hadn't yet gone into a gay bar feeling like a piece of meat. He hadn't had random sexual encounters with guys where he felt guilty and impure. It was like he was an untouched gay and I had found him. I wanted him all to myself.

THE '90S BAR

MY INFATUATION INTENSIFIED as I continued meeting up with Craig throughout the summer. I was living a fantasy. His chest and thick arms bulged out of his tight white polo shirt that accentuated his dark tan. When we entered restaurants, I could see bartenders, servers, patrons all stop and follow him with their eyes. It was like he was my trophy.

We had one fantasy weekend after another. Since we lived apart, we would meet in various cities. Vail. New York. Milwaukee. I was beginning to feel like I was on The Bachelor. Living in some augmented reality without any normal dates in the same city as most people do. But instead of meeting up with someone open and free, I was with someone whose emotional maturity was damaged.

Each weeknight, between our once-a-month weekend get-aways, I sat alone on my couch in my living room watching TV and I couldn't stop thinking about Craig. And like a song that I couldn't stop replaying over and over, my logical mind would continuously fixate on the large, obvious red flags.

I thought back to one of the weekends we had shared in New York. We had planned a fun evening of dancing to '90s music at a dive bar a few blocks away from our dinner location. The 2017 Women's March around the world had taken place earlier in the day. I should have known better than asking what he thought about the march since it was a trending topic for both political parties, but I was hopeful that just maybe he would have something positive to say about it.

But the hope was dead on arrival. Craig launched into a diatribe about the march and his annoyed tone instantly pierced through our once intimate, playful mood. The moment was an all-too-common series of events for us. One of us would tentatively bring up a contested political topic with the hopes of finding common ground. And every time, it didn't matter who brought up the topic, the other would tend to disagree.

He passionately explained his position that the Women's March was not about women's rights but only designed to drag down President Donald Trump, whom he supported. But it became obvious that he wasn't able to put himself in the shoes of the marchers to understand their strife. To understand what they were fighting for or even why they were motivated to fight. He only could see one side. His side.

As I was listening to him pitch his steadfast political viewpoint, the thought smacked me across the face: Craig had never gone through any adversity in his life. No struggle of class, caste, race, sexuality, or religion. He was a white, "straight," Catholic male who grew up in a white, middle-class suburban neighborhood, just like me. But he didn't know what it was like to struggle to understand his sexual identity during his formative years. To be a societal outcast.

In the back of my mind, it became obvious that Craig's coming-out journey would be even more complex than I had originally thought. To admit that he was gay would be admitting he was a minority. That he would be viewed differently by others. And he would have to go through adversity, something that typically is learned in the formative years of our lives. Which made me wonder how a thirty-something would ever overcome this.

Our awkward conversation followed us out into the cold, windy evening. The busy street was jammed with traffic as we walked down the sidewalk littered with people finding their way through the East Village.

As I tried to articulate my views, Craig's aggressive and defensive tone began to repress any thoughts that I had. My mind and heart began to shutter. My once-hopeful attitude to engage in a healthy conversation turned into disappointment and sadness. And as I shut down, the anger bubbling inside of him made his face swell.

My fingers, ears, and toes were numb as we arrived at the '90s bar in silence. The lively, roaring music rolled out of the hinged bar door as patrons' liquid encouragement allowed them to carelessly sing aloud to the nostalgic tunes.

As we stood shivering in front of the bar door, I suggested we put our uncomfortable conversation on the back burner and try to enjoy the remaining portion of the evening that we had both been looking forward to. Infuriated, Craig told me that he didn't like the look in my eyes when I was explaining myself earlier. He said it scared him that I didn't know him very well.

It quickly became apparent that we wouldn't be able to salvage any part of the rest of the night. Our meltdown was too much to overcome and enter the bar. The sounds of '90s music echoed past me as I had no choice but to hail a cab.

I looked out of the steamy cab window as the towering buildings skidded by on our way back to the hotel. Thoughts of my mother enduring her marriage for 34 years crept into my mind. How she sacrificed her life for better or for worse, compromising a portion of her happiness as a result. And how she eventually wasn't able to break through to her partner to help teach him how to love.

The cab's tires rumbled over the bumps and cracks as it maneuvered through the busy avenue, breaking up the interior silence in the back seat. I knew that I couldn't continue the familial pattern I had witnessed. My instinct to help others and fix problems was activated. Something I so badly wanted to do for Craig. But

I knew in my gut that I had to instead apply my mother's life lesson. I had to find a way to be me.

GUT INSTINCT

WHAT I THOUGHT wouldn't last the summer had gone on nearly two years when we found ourselves in New Paltz, New York, on yet another romantic getaway. After weeks of anxious rumination, I finally built up the courage to ask Craig as we lay relaxing in the cozy bed at a historic Inn, only this time it was Valentine's Day. "When are you going to ask me?"

Craig rolled his shirtless body onto his side on the pure white comforter to look at me as he held up his head with his hand. His eyes squinted and he paused, acting as if he was caught off guard. But now that we were a couple years into our relationship, he knew that I was waiting for him to actually say the word "boyfriend." I could have forced the issue a while ago, but I wanted to hear it from him. He needed to be ready to say it. And I knew that if he could refer to me as his boyfriend, that he could begin to come out to himself.

"I've thought about it a lot, but I am not ready. It scares me to get into another relationship so fast since I am just getting out of one," he said as he looked down. His body language loudly revealed that he couldn't bring himself to say the word. "I am concerned that not being ready will hurt you and it may take a long time for me to get there." He looked up and peered back into my eyes. The rest of his words were quiet. "I think you could do better than me right now."

I could hear the screaming voice in my gut, "Run now. Run far, far away." Where were my little gray alien friends from the spaceship? Couldn't they just come down and smack me? To wake me up and help me cut the cord now? But my heart remained paralyzed. I wanted him to want me. To work through everything and fight to keep me. The past two years of sharing special moments were almost impossible to dismiss. I couldn't think of our time together as something that would *end*.

"What does your gut tell you?" I cautiously asked him. "Does it say you should be on your own to figure it out? Maybe I am just holding you back from figuring it all out." My gut was telling me that he should be out there on his own as a single gay guy like I had done when I first came out. Experiencing his own sexuality to figure out what he didn't want, which would help him understand what he does. But my ego couldn't accept the idea of letting him go. Even the thought of him going out to gay bars alone made me jealous. I could just see him walking through the door and everyone's eyes pouncing him like he was fresh meat.

"My gut tells me that I should be on my own to figure it out," he said. My heart sank. But I knew this is what he needed. "You are an amazing catch. I enjoy all the time I spend with you," he continued.

Even though I gave him an out to follow his gut and be on his own that Valentine's Day, we weren't ready to admit defeat from love and decided to remain a couple. And while we chose to avoid the painful emotional path, we knew deep in our guts that no matter how hard we tried, our paths diverging was inevitable.

DRUG OF CHOICE

As I SAT in the back row of seats, I looked out across the amphitheater of one of largest interior spaces at PepsiCo's corporate headquarters and could see all of the presidents of each global division sitting in the first couple rows below. The entire Executive Committee was on display, donned in their impressive corporate attire, anticipating the annual employee recognition ceremony, which recognized the company's best employees from around the world, celebrating one of the highest levels of achievement an employee could earn.

As the ceremony began, I thought back to earlier in the day when I had flown back from Florida from a mini-vacation with my family. Craig was supposed have been there with us, but he and I had taken one of our many breaks apart from each other. After several days of introspective thinking, I still couldn't make up my mind what I wanted to do. Craig was like a drug. When I was with him, I was on a high. But when I wasn't with him, I was the lowest of lows.

But as time went on, I began to develop a sense of loneliness when I was with him. As if I were better off alone. It became apparent that most of what we had in common were all things at the surface level. While all the outward signs led to smiles and laughter, I began to feel deep inner feelings of unhappiness. I began to lose myself.

My body flinched when I heard the Chief Executive Officer call my name from on stage. I quickly snapped out of my depressed stupor as the audience turned to look around the room to locate the award winner. As I stood up, a glowing sense of pride washed away my uneasiness. I quickly buttoned my navy-blue suit coat and made my way to the aisle.

As I took each step closer to the main stage, I could feel the appreciation from all of PepsiCo's top executives staring back at me as they clapped for my achievement. My work creating and leading Global Ally Day helped me reach a pinnacle of success that I had worked so hard to achieve.

I stepped up into the bright lights shining down on stage while the onlooking crowd continued to applaud. And as my hand connected with one of the most recognized CEOs in the world, the irony exploded in my head. It had instantly occurred to me that while I was accepting an award and being recognized for successfully helping LGBT+ employees around the world become their authentic selves in the workplace, I was dating someone who wasn't ready to come out to himself.

It was like I was violating everything I had been working hard to do to help others. It felt like most things in my life were successfully flowing, but one huge piece was stunted. I was so close to becoming me. I was so close, yet I had chosen not to be.

THE LAST CLOSET

THE LATE AFTERNOON sun slowly began to sink. As the temperature began to drop, the lazy crowd of beachgoers sparsely sitting about the white sand beach began to casually pack up the space they had occupied all day.

Craig and I lay side by side, motionless, on the oversized lawn blanket. The soft sand under the blanket shifted around to create the perfect body cradle for the afternoon. As the light wind caressed my resting face, my eyes casually drifted open and closed with the faint sounds of the calm waves lapping up on shore about thirty yards away.

I wanted to feel all the romantic and intimate vibes created by the placid ambiance. But the serene sensations were juxtaposed against the unhappiness my soul delicately harbored. My heart had remained overwhelmed with emotion since I decided to give the relationship yet another try months ago. And the relentless feeling in my gut had now overpowered my heart.

I rolled over onto my side facing Craig as the light breeze began to chill my exposed skin. Craig felt my small shift on the blanket and awoke from a brief snooze. As his eyes adjusted to the fading light, he rolled over on his side to face me.

The weather was so perfect that we weren't quite ready to leave. Most people had now left the beach and it felt like we had the entire span of beautiful sand to ourselves. I looked into his eyes and tried to feel my loving soul. My fading heart wanted so badly for him to be the one. But it was time to finally come out and say it out loud.

We began chatting about our weeks ahead. I was excited for him, as he was so close to earning a spot on his company's upcoming annual award trip. It always made me happy to see his passion shine through when he talked about his success. His eyes would light up and I could feel his energy as he outlined his personal strategy. I was proud to see him proud.

"So when you win your spot on the Hawaii trip, would you bring me along?" I asked with a cheeky smile on my face. Even though it came out as a rhetorical question, my subconscious mind knew that it was a reasonable ask. I thought about dropping the conversation, but I was instantly curious with what he would say.

He paused, taking in what I had asked. "Well, yeah," he responded. But after he responded, it was like everything that began flowing out of my mouth had been pre-meditated. I explained my random question, comparing it to my cousin, who was a successful sales representative who attended many sales-related award trips, and I knew she always brought her boyfriend along with her.

But as I walked through the entire flow of the award trip in my mind, I could naturally visualize Craig's personal dilemma unexpectedly materializing. What would I be to Craig? How would Craig introduce me to top executives of the company at the numerous events and dinners that couples attend together?

I could feel the conversation leading into a very awkward space as I probed a little further. Either Craig was acting naive or truly wasn't sure where I was going with the conversation. But either way, my heart needed to hear his answer.

"When you introduce me to your work colleagues, would you say, 'This is my boyfriend, Cory' or would you say, 'This is my friend, Cory'?"

Craig's eyes squinted and his lips tightened. He shook his head slightly and without much hesitation he said, "I would tell them that you were my friend. Why?"

I wasn't able to deliver an answer as the lump in my throat tightened while I tried to swallow. I shut my eyes and thought back through thirty months of effort that I had invested into our relationship to only be considered a friend. Silence fell as the sun began to drift below the horizon. I felt alone.

The once-warm air turned cooler with each passing minute. Goosebumps appeared all over my skin. My heart wanted to believe Craig was capable of a smoother life pivot. But my gut finally punched me. I had already come out of many closets. And I didn't need to come out of any more. I finally had succumbed. He had to be him. And I had to be me.

8
I ALMOST BECAME ME

J ust down the hall from the executive boardroom, I was watching the past six months of my hard work play out live on a big screen TV hung up on a wall of the windowless audio-visual room. Even though I had orchestrated the entire Board of Directors presentation, I wasn't senior enough to be inside of the actual boardroom.

On the screen, the leader of PepsiCo's global beverages group stood at the front of the room and introduced everyone to the detailed presentation of our five-year global strategy. A sense of pride bubbled inside of me that was frequently interrupted with bursts of nervousness pulsing through my stomach and chest.

The boardroom was on the top floor of the executive building at PepsiCo's World Headquarters just north of New York City. Large windows took up two sides of the corner office that overlooked the corporate sculpture garden scattered throughout the vast, perfectly manicured green lawn. A jumbo LED screen bordered by turbosound speakers built into wall took up the entire front wall of the room.

The long, horseshoe-shaped, wooden boardroom table was lined all the way around the outside edge with sleek, modern office chairs made with a soft, elastic mesh material. White name cards with black block letters were placed in front of each seat so everyone knew who each person was. Small, quarter-sized microphones were embedded into the beautiful, light-colored wood at each position to capture each executive's words in the oversized conference room.

Current and former CEOs and CFOs of Fortune 50 companies sat among the professionally dressed team of PepsiCo's Board of Directors in the executive boardroom. PepsiCo's global leadership team, led by the CEO, filled the remaining seats around the table and benches along the backside of the room. A full house for one of the most important meetings of the year at one of the world's leading food and beverage companies.

We had carefully choreographed the day-long presentation and now it was showtime. Sizzle videos. Innovative new product tastings. Fresh ice chests full of our chilled products shipped in from around the world. Swag bags. Breakthrough solutions to new consumer trends. Glitzy marketing plans. An eight-hour, multi-sensory stimulation masterpiece.

As the head of the global beverages group stood in his expensive suit, donned with a bright pink pocket square, and confidently delivered his pitch, my mind drifted back through the past six months. I weaved in and out of the countless conversations I had with top executives around the world to craft a bullet-proof five-year strategy for the beverages category in each region of the globe. Products that will eventually be consumed by billions of people around the planet every day. A wave of chills flowed across my skin knowing that I helped pull all of this together.

BALLER DAYDREAMS

TWO MONTHS EARLIER, I walked out of the exclusive-use terminal and onto the private jet tarmac area of the Westchester County Airport in New York. I began to suppress the giddiness I felt so others could see that I was all business. That I played the part of a company executive as I was about to board the company's private jet alongside the head of our global beverages group and other beverages group colleagues.

My navy-blue blazer flapped in the wind on the chilly Friday morning in March. My weekend bag had been loaded into the cargo hold at the back of the plane by a well-dressed staff member of the corporate jet company. I carried my black laptop bag up the narrow, retractable stairs leading into jet. I turned the corner once I was through the doorway and began walking through the plane's single-aisle interior lined with shiny mahogany finishes. My eyes couldn't fully contain my excitement. I felt like a baller.

It was understood that the first four cream-colored leather seats, two on each side facing each other that could swivel 360 degrees once airborne, were dedicated to the top executives on the flight. The three other colleagues and I who were lower in the group's pecking order made our way to the next set of four leather chairs in the back just past the small dining area. Another lounge with benches on both sides that converted into a queen-sized bed was located behind the main section with a full bathroom at the very back of the aircraft.

I peered out of the oversized oval window as the ground slowly fell away from us. The sun lit up the houses neatly plotted along the neighborhood roads eventually turning into forests and thickets as we thrust forward.

As I sat in the cushy leather seat, I remembered my younger, carefree self lying on the warm, green grass of my childhood home staring up into the blue sky. I would spot small dots in the sky effortlessly drifting across the perfectly blue canvas. With a grin on my boyish face, my mind played out scenarios that one day I would be up there in the airplane looking toward the ground, wondering if someone was looking up at the airplane that I was flying in. I dreamed of jetting off to far-away places in a private jet. And now at 35,000 feet, it felt like my childhood daydreams had come true.

"Are you ready, Cory?" the head of the global beverages group called out from the seats up front. My head twitched, pulling me out of my nostalgic daydream. I reached down into my laptop bag and pulled out two hundred pages of thick paper clipped together by an oversized binder clip. It was go time.

While the primary purpose of the weekend trip was for the team to enjoy themselves in Austin at the SXSW festival, this didn't apply to me. My primary task for the weekend was to present our team's initial draft of the Board of Directors' presentation to the head of the global beverages group on the flight to Austin. Then, over the weekend, I would need to work virtually with my strategy colleagues back in New York to have a near final draft back to him on the return flight on Sunday.

As I listened to the flowing feedback from the head of the global beverages group towards the front of the plane, my pen swiftly made annotations. It became difficult to keep up with the onslaught of real-time corrections and additional analyses that needed to be chartered to help tell the story. But there was no pause for me to catch up. Mental notes carefully placed in my mind to help remember what needed to happen with each page that I needed to log once our brief meeting ended. It quickly became apparent that my weekend in Austin would be spent in front of my laptop.

But this was on par for the role I had been promoted into. This was corporate America. This is what I had signed up for. And I was nailing it. Predicting. Coordinating. Analyzing. Proving. Collaborating. Resolving. Uncovering. Creating. Discussing. Selling. Choreographing. Performing.

Not only was I new to the strategy function, but I was also new to the entire executive team in New York after transferring from Chicago just six months earlier. Learning personalities. Figuring out how to navigate my way through the corporate politics. Understanding the executive players. Presenting to the highest level.

BREADCRUMB TREASURE HUNT

AS THE HEAD of the global beverages group continued to deliver the strategy that I helped create to PepsiCo's Board of Directors, I took a moment to close my eyes and feel my sense of accomplishment. A grin slowly filled my face as I looked up at the television screen. A divine sense of pride began flowing through me. Everything that I had pushed for to get to this point in my life, every position that I held throughout my career, had prepared me for this moment. I was at the pinnacle of my career.

I heard the sizzle videos play uplifting beats accompanying the exciting visuals on the screen creating euphoric harmony. I saw the nonverbal satisfaction emanating from each executive sitting around the table as they intently listened. I felt the pure bliss of success. All of the hard work and all of the long hours were playing out in front of my eyes.

The emotional high lasted for several weeks after the milestone meeting. But after the buzz went away, a feeling of emptiness began to creep back into my mind. And it wasn't an emptiness as a result of the project. It was a deeper emptiness.

I had certainly created success for myself. And isn't success what we strive for in our lives? Success that we have personally created? This, then, becomes the pinnacle of our career or of our life?

Over the course of my life, I envisioned life was all about the success that I created. But it became more and more apparent through these collective moments that maybe there was more to life than the artificial success that I felt was necessary to strive for.

It began to feel like the Board of Directors' project was something to keep my mind occupied for a moment of my life. Like it was just another corporate task to satisfy my hunger for the feeling of success. The only thing that remained after the project was six months of paychecks, commiserating stories with colleagues, and another line item added to my resume.

The project didn't turn into a positive memory that I would share with my family. In fact, I am sure my family and friends were sick of hearing about the project. The more I began to think about how the past six months fit into my life, it began to feel that it was a time filler. Just a means to an end.

It became apparent that the feeling of success was temporary. Just like the other corporate achievements I have had throughout my successful career. The achievements were merely breadcrumbs for me, breadcrumbs that temporarily satisfied a hunger to find out who I was. Sure, I could keep eating the breadcrumbs. And I could continue the adventure of this breadcrumb treasure hunt. But what was truly at the end of the path that I was on?

As it played out over and over in my mind, I realized the treasure at the end of this path was a retirement party. A toast to a great contributor to an organization selling soda and chips. A look back over a successful resume. Of all the return on investment numbers. Of all the quarterly earnings reports of 5% year-over-year growth. Of the annual reviews of "exceeds expectations." Of the promotions and bonuses and stock options.

Each year, a new door would be opened to reveal a new shiny object that I couldn't refuse. Each shiny object led me down the same predictable path—one that ends with me looking back at my years of unhappiness, something that I wouldn't realize until the years were gone.

THE ALIEN WHACK

THE SUNDAY AFTERNOON sunshine caressed my skin. The long row of slatted wooden benches bordered the pathway that followed the edge of the serene pond lined with colorful water lilies and other blooming aquatic plants. I sat with my legs extended and with both arms outstretched in the middle of an empty bench, gazing out at the small rowboats that dotted the large pond.

As I took in a breath of the fresh air, my gaze flowed from the large weeping willow trees that effortlessly hung over the far edges of the pond and up into the majestic, multi-level masterpieces that jutted far into the sky bordering the western edge of the Park. Distinct and exclusive towers rich in history that have been Central Park landmarks for centuries.

This is my spot. One of my favorite places in New York City. A place where I have sat for hours countless times before: thinking, meditating, daydreaming, writing, crying, being. A place I discovered two days after September 11, 2001, when I left my Midtown East apartment and solemnly walked to the Park. A place

I always go back to. An urban retreat surrounded by an island of chaos yet creating a blissful space where my mind was able to flow, unforced.

Three months had passed since the Board of Directors presentation and I was struggling with my job. As my body soaked in the warmth from the sun, my eyes drifted closed. Calm conversations of passersby began to give way to a peaceful silence. I entered the euphoric state of flow and my life came into distinct focus. I visualized each piece of the large, complicated puzzle flawlessly fitting together. The meticulous resume that I had consciously designed. The years of unconsciously being.

I thought back to becoming Student Government president at Ball State University, landing a job on Wall Street, being selected for the highly coveted derivatives position out of a training class filled with Ivy-Leaguers, climbing the corporate ladder at a Fortune 50 company and then landing a position in the prestigious strategy group, a group where only top-level strategy consultants from top, global consulting firms like McKinsey & Company or Bain & Company are placed.

Out of nowhere, the sun that once warmed the top of my eyelids became instantly blocked. My eyes flashed open to see the circular alien spaceship hovering overhead. Deja vu overtook my mind. Green and yellow lights blinked along the bottom of the humming, shiny metallic structure that appeared to be spinning counterclockwise. A loud noise that sounded like pressure being released from a soda can was followed by the circular opening at the center of the spacecraft swinging open, sending out a dense white fog. A bright, artificial yellow tubular light instantly beamed down on me.

I froze. My eyes transfixed upward as my head was cocked back and I saw a huge pair of eyes sitting atop the small-framed, gray creature appearing out of the thick fog. Its body swiftly floated down before it hovered several feet in front of me. Its large creamy white eyes blinked and a happy grin spread out across its tiny mouth. Like it was about to tell me something.

WHACK! Just like that, its tiny little hand came out of nowhere and smacked me on the side of my head. I could feel the coarse, wrinkled skin of its miniature hand on my earlobe. Its grin turned into a beaming smile and after a warm gaze into my eyes with one last blink, the creature flashed upward into the spaceship. The center opening swung shut and the spaceship vanished into the blue sky without any time to process what was happening.

That was it. It all somehow clicked. Without even trying to understand how it happened, I had completed the puzzle. I had proven that I could do anything that I wanted to do up to this point of my life. A pattern came into plain sight. Like it had just floated down and landed in my mind's eye. It had been right there in front of me the entire time. But I just had to see it. I just had to realize it.

I had proven that I could be successful at most anything I chose to do, even if I wasn't passionate about it. I had planned my entire career to get to this point and I became successful at each stage of my career. But it turns out that I didn't truly love what I was doing. Being successful and loving what you do are two very different things. Which meant, if I could use all of that energy toward something that I was passionate about, then there was no doubt that I would be successful.

And that is why I never felt like I was me. I kept almost becoming me. But I never would be me unless I followed my true passion. What was in my being to do. It wasn't about accomplishments. It wasn't about other people. It was about happiness.

ENTERING EUPHORIA

SIX MONTHS HAD passed. I walked out into the morning gripping my cell phone. I crossed over the avenue that ran along the beach and began to make my way toward the water. Even though the sun had risen about an hour ago, the bright rays were still reflecting off of the beautiful dark blue waters on the horizon.

The warm sea breeze lightly tickled my skin as it rushed past. There is something about the fresh ocean air that immediately puts me at ease. Maybe it is a combination of hearing the calm waves lapping up on the white sand or of the moist, salty fragrance that enters my nose with each inhale. But with each deep breath, my soul became closer to peaceful harmony.

The soft blades of grass caressed the soles of my bare feet as they slid across the large green lawn. Each slow, progressive step became meditative, helping calm the nerves in my chest. My phone should ring in ten minutes, which gave me enough time to find a place to sit and relax my mind. We had agreed this would be the best time to have the call since it was a sixteen-hour time difference between New York and Sydney.

I walked across the small parking area and descended the concrete stairway leading down to the pure white sand that had been neatly groomed over the night.

Stunning, commissioned graffiti-scapes covered the large seawall that lined the back of the famous beach. The soft sand massaged my feet as I made my way over to an empty bench positioned in front of the colorful, iconic seawall. I sat down, made sure my ringer was set to vibrate mode, and took a long, deep breath in to cleanse my lungs.

Many people were out performing their morning routines. Runners on the sand. Dog walkers taking in the beautiful morning with their pals. A few surfers hovering on their boards, waiting for the perfect morning wave. Birds overhead calling out as they floated by. My eyes twinkled at the blissful setting painted before me.

My back straight, my shoulders relaxed, my gaze on the glistening horizon, I began to fill my lungs with the ocean air. After I couldn't take in any more air, I slowly let go of my breath, letting the warm air escape. My eyelids softly closed. My body softened further and my mind became clearer and clearer with each slow breath.

Within a couple of minutes, the soothing ocean waves and other sounds around me melted away. I felt like I was floating. Nothing in the world mattered at that moment. The nervous feeling that I felt several minutes ago had dissolved. With a happy smile, my face relaxed and a euphoric sensation coated my exposed skin and then penetrated my entire being. My tranquil mind began replaying the actions of the past five months that had changed my life forever. And my life-changing story was still being written.

THE MOMENT OF TRUTH

MY EYES FLIPPED open into the darkness. The light from the city below illuminated my white bedroom ceiling. I blinked several times, trying to get my mind to catch up to my sudden alertness. I rolled over and glanced at my phone. 3:03 am. Maybe it was the time change from flying back from Bali yesterday, but my mind was racing.

I had thought back to my experience over the past couple weeks and my life-changing encounter with a girl from Paris at one of the most famous open-air yoga studios in the world. I sat on a picnic table under a canopy hearing her talk about how she had just grabbed her life by the balls. How she bravely left everything she knew in France, including her corporate marketing job, and followed her passion to learn to be a yoga instructor in Bali. How she would figure out her life without worry.

I realized my two-week vacation was not enough to heal my soul. To heal my longing to follow my passions in life. My gut was speaking loudly. It was time to be 100% happy. It was time to give into my fears.

I pushed myself up in my bed, rolled to the edge, and placed my feet on the cool, hardwood floor. As my eyes continued to adjust to the darkened surroundings, the word 'sabbatical' instantly flashed across my mind's eye. Thinking back to a conversation several months ago I had with a colleague, I remembered her saying that her previous consulting firm required short-term sabbaticals for each of their employees, preventing corporate burnout.

I walked out into my living room and pulled out my laptop from my backpack. I placed the computer on my dining table and the glow of the screen softly lit up my face as the device powered on. After I was unable to find anything labeled "sabbatical" in my company's benefits website, my squinting eyes lit up a few moments later. There it was on the screen: "Leave of Absence." I proceeded to read the policy that stated any employee could leave their current position, taking up to six months of unpaid leave, and still receive benefits with the approval of their manager and human resources representative.

Little did I realize at the time that those simple actions would set into motion a new chapter in my life that I once only dreamed of. Something that took many, many years to build up enough confidence to enact. And it all happened so quickly. I met with the human resources representative the same day, who was extremely supportive and encouraging. My manager, a longtime strategist who believed in me enough to hire me into the strategy group, told me that he would help with whatever I needed.

The leave-of-absence paperwork was signed in a couple of days, and three weeks later, my six-month break away from my job at PepsiCo began. After some quick maneuvering, I had successfully broken my two-year lease with my landlord and moved all of my belongings into a storage unit. I didn't know what would happen over the next six months. No rent. No debt. No address. It was the first time in my career that I did not have a plan.

And so it began without hesitation. I took a last-minute trip to Antarctica, achieving my quest to step foot on all seven continents before the age of fifty. Done. Largest waterfall system in the world in Argentina. Check. Beautiful beaches on the southern edge of the Caribbean Sea in Colombia. Yes, please. Ziplining in Costa Rica. Road trip to visit friends in Florida. Why not?

OWNING MY DESTINY

THE WINDSHIELD WIPERS on my car struggled to catch up as the rain pelted my windshield while I drove through Alabama on my way to Florida. The radio dialed into a local rock station. My eyes fixated on the white lines of the highway and the cars in front of me. As the rain let up slightly, the song Sweet Home Alabama began playing on the speakers. I turned the song up so I could sing even louder, easing my concern about the tough driving conditions.

With both hands gripping the steering wheel, I noticed out of the corner of my eye that my phone lit up. I quickly slipped my headphones into my ears and turned down the radio. I recognized the number, but wondered why PepsiCo would be calling me out of the blue only a couple months into my leave of absence.

My mind instantly shifted back to why I had to take a leave of absence. And why I couldn't have just left the company outright to begin my new life. The feeling of being trapped overcame me. I knew that I would have to come back to my job after my leave of absence was over. My executive relocation package that helped me move to New York required me to stay with the company for at least two more years to avoid paying back a lot of moving expenses that I had already incurred.

But I knew that I was ready to leave the company now. The leave of absence had given me a taste of what I so desperately wanted. The time away from the office began opening up the blinders. It helped me see that I could leave and I would be ok. That I would find a way to live on my own.

It was difficult to hear her voice through the pounding rain, but the human resources representative began to explain over the phone that she wanted to check in to see how I was doing. To see how I was enjoying my time away. But as she continued with the conversation and through her questioning, it became apparent that she was fishing around for some information about my future plans.

My face softened and I grinned. I had been waiting for this moment for a long time. Prior to embarking on my leave of absence, one of my strategy colleagues was assigned a large but secret project. A project to reorganize the company that would most likely be announced while I was still on my leave. As many in the corporate world are aware, these company shifts typically play out every two to three years. And the shifts consist of department reorganizations requiring position eliminations, a way for the company to save money and cut costs.

The careful and calculated verbal choreography flowed through my mouth. But it was my honest, heartfelt words that sealed the deal. I knew that if my position was eliminated, my relocation contract to New York the previous year would most likely be released.

I told her that if my relocation contract didn't exist, I probably wouldn't come back to the company after my leave of absence. Not really surprised, she thanked me for being honest. Even though it was sort of an awkward call, I knew that I had just written myself out of the company.

LETTING GO

THE LIGHT BREEZE gently pulled the warm moisture against my face bringing my mind back to the serene setting as I remained motionless on the bench. The sound of the waves fifty yards in front of me swished into my ears. My breaths had deepened. A final exhale fully reset any nerves that had built up inside.

It was Valentine's Day. One year ago, I was lying with my ex-boyfriend, trying to find a way to make our relationship work. But today, I was sitting on a bench watching the sun warmly greet everyone moving about the Australian beach. Everyone was in a pure beach state of mind. My phone began to vibrate. I turned it over and saw they were right on time.

"Hi Cory," the human resources representative said. "We are sorry to inform you that your position with PepsiCo has been eliminated. We will provide you with the resources you need in your severance package," she explained. My manager was also on the call to thank me for my years of service. The call was brief and to the point. I politely thanked them for letting me know.

I switched the phone off and placed it into my pocket. My gaze at the ocean's horizon softened. My skin began to tingle. My chest became heavy. Even though I had expected this would be the outcome, warm tears rolled out of my eyes and moistened my cheeks.

But as I sat in peace with my mind empty, I could feel a sense of joy that I hadn't felt in a long time. A deeper feeling of happiness.

For the first time in my life, I had set myself free. I finally had let go. I let go of all the questions that I was afraid to answer. Questions like, "How will I make money if I left my job?", "How will I save for retirement?", and "How will I afford healthcare?"

I had always told myself that I wanted to have all of the answers before I let go. But I finally let go without knowing.

This was my life and I was living it. But most importantly, I was actually being me. Everything I had done was me all along; I just hadn't realized it yet. Every decision, every action, every thought. I had been me the entire time.

It was time for me to accept me as I am, to realize that this is the one life I have. And I should live each day with purpose.

The sun is getting higher now, the air warmer. I stretch out my arms and lean back, looking up at the blue sky. A wide smile appears on my calm face. I press my feet into the warm sand. My surfing lesson begins in thirty minutes and it is time to walk to the surf shop across the beach to pick up my board.

A new journey awaits.

◇

Thank you for buying this book!

I would appreciate your feedback on what chapters helped you most, and what you would like to see in future books.

If you enjoyed this book and found it helpful, please leave a REVIEW on Amazon.

Visit my personal page at www.corycalvin.com where you can sign up for email updates about my upcoming books and transformational businesses.

Connect with me directly by email: cory@corycalvin.com

Thank you!

◇

Made in the USA
Middletown, DE
30 May 2019